the chapter of the self

The Buddhist Society Trust is a distinguished press in the United Kingdom which enriches lives around the world by advancing the study and practice of Buddhism.

Its activities are supported by charitable contributions from individuals and institutions.

For more information visit: info@thebuddhistsociety.org

First published by Routledge & Kegan Paul Ltd., London, 1978
Second edition published by by The Buddhist Society Trust, 2018

The publisher gratefully acknowledges the generous contribution to this book provided by The Trevor Leggett Adhyatma Yoga Trust and Dr Desmond Biddulph CBE for his generous support and encouragement.

The Buddhist Society Trust
E: middlewayandpublishing@gmail.com

ISBN: 978–0–901032–52–2 (The Buddhist Society Trust)

A catalogue record for this book is available from the British Library

Edited by Sarah Auld
Designed by Avni Patel

Printed in Padstow, Cornwall by TJ International

the chapter of the self

Yoga and the Discovery of the Universal Self

Trevor Leggett

Nilakantha: a peak just north of Badrinath where Shankara founded a monastery. (Courtesy of the Japanese-Indian Nanda Devi Expedition)

To the late Dr Hari Prasad Shastri,
Pandit and Jnani of India,
these translations and transcriptions
are reverently dedicated.

Contents

Introduction

THIS BOOK PRESENTS an ancient Sanskrit text dealing with self-realisation, God-realisation and yoga, aiming at a radical and permanent change of the individual consciousness, which as it stands is limited by a sort of illusion. It is the kind of illusion experienced by a man dreaming of a terrifying lion whose roars are in fact his own snoring, or by people who faint at *Dracula*, or grip their seats in panic at a Cinerama.

The texts of realisation may not dispel illusion if the mind that receives them is clouded and only partially attentive; the methods of making it clear and effortlessly one-pointed are called, collectively, yoga.

Realisation is its own goal, but yoga is a means.

As a means, yoga can be used fractionally to acquire some imagined advantages in life as it now is. But these are temporary, and do not confront the ultimate problem. They correspond to improving the circumstances of a dream. Isolated yogic methods can be used to give some calmness, or improve health, or produce vigour. One who is prepared to practise hard can make the mind and memory brilliant. But if these seeming advantages are in the service of a fundamental illusion, there is no lasting peace; and in a disturbed mind, the temporary gains arouse waves of excitement which in the end destroy the yoga practice itself.

Texts like this one have often been translated, and studied, by Western (and some Eastern) scholars who are interested in the philosophy in them; the references to yoga practice are brushed aside as superstition or self-hypnosis. The worldview of some of the ancient texts has sometimes been admired, though only as a remarkable anticipation of some modern views, and in any case merely as a system of ideas. Self-realisation is thought of as an intellectual conviction, somehow held as an 'insight' in the teeth of actual experience.

Thus many presentations of the ancient teachings concentrate on only one part: philosophy alone, or yoga practice alone. Pure scholars ignore the yoga practices and religious devotions which appear in the texts; to them yoga is in the same category as Chinese acupuncture until a few years ago – something was known about it, but it never occurred to anyone that it might be worth investigating. On the other hand, those interested in yogic exercises give no attention to the texts which say clearly that exercises alone will merely reinforce the illusion which is the cause of all man's frustrations.

Philosophy alone is sterile; yoga alone is a tightening tangle.

The basic texts were composed long before the Christian era, but all the threads were drawn together by the great teacher Shankara, in about A.D. 700. His writings have been elaborately studied, but mainly for the brilliant synthesis of the texts on self-realisation; his writings on yoga practice have mostly been ignored. There has been a view that no intelligent man could believe in it, so Shankara could not have believed it either, but was merely making concessions to the orthodoxies of his time. A word like samadhi, which to him is a trance where there is only one pre-determined thought and complete absence of sense-perception, has been translated merely as 'intentness' or 'without wayward thoughts', and his whole position presented as merely intellectual.

But Shankara saw himself not as propounding a theoretical world-view, but as teaching a change of consciousness. His aim is to go beyond individuality, through realisation of the ancient truths by means of yogic meditation. Again and again in his Gita commentary he says that meditation on truth is the direct means to knowledge. Just over twenty years ago [in the early 1950s – Ed.], a commentary by him on the textbook of yoga practice, *The Yoga Sutras of Patanjali*, was discovered, which to the surprise of some scholars has passed the tests of authenticity [this is still the subject of some academic debate – Ed.].

The purpose of the present book is to present both sides of Shankara's teaching. Rather than re-translate parts of his known works, I have set myself to put before those interested one short authentic work, the commentary on the Chapter of the Self in the Apastamba Law-book, which as far as I know has not appeared in English.

In this commentary, he repeatedly refers to the role of yoga practice, but does not discuss in this place the methods. So I have added Part Two, on the practice of his yoga, which I studied for eighteen years with Dr Hari Prasad Shastri, a great scholar and a fully realised yogi. Dr Shastri often used traditional stories as a method of instruction, and told his pupils also to study the working of yogic principles in history. I have included a number of traditional stories here.

Also included is a good deal of the newly discovered Shankara commentary on the Yoga Sutras, which I believe will be new in English. Dr Shastri himself lectured on these sutras for two years; however he stressed, as a most faithful follower of Shankara, that yoga practice must be based on the revelations of truth, or it will not give freedom.

NOTE ON SANSKRIT WORDS

In the body of the book, Sanskrit words are given in approximate Anglicised forms, sometimes grammatically anomalous. For example, the established words yogi and Nirvana should be: either yogin and Nirvana, or else yogi and Nirvanam. (There should be a macron over the first 'a' and a dot under the second 'n' of Nirvana – Nirvāṇa.) But these words are established in English; experience shows that diacritical marks do not long survive transplantation into a foreign language. The inconsistency and general looseness of the Anglicised forms may be distressing, though only to those who know how the words ought strictly to be rendered; but countless examples show that when a field of theory and practice is carried from one language to another, there has to be some accommodation. Technical terms have to be retained when there is no proper equivalent; it is also useless to spell names by some elaborate system. No one writes yogī or Jūdō, and not many would go to a Čaykovskij concert. So in general I write Shankara and not Śaṅkara or Çaṃkara, and similarly with other words.

But as the translation of the Chapter of the Self commentary is new, one of the standard systems of transliteration is used in that section, and in the appendices. Readers must be prepared to find Śaṅkara and other unfamiliar spellings there.

HOW TO USE THIS BOOK FOR YOGA PRACTICE

Make up your mind to give the practices a fair test for six weeks. You will have to learn enough theory for a working background. The following sections of part one will give a useful basis:

THEORY:
Read chapter 1 – the sacred texts.
Read chapters 2 and 3 – the Law–book and Chapter of the Self.
Read chapter 4 – Shankara the Teacher.

PRACTICE:
Read chapter 8 – Outline of Practice.
Traditionally, it is recommended to do spiritual practice in the morning shortly after rising before taking up the cares of the day.
Establish the seat (page 85).
Read a holy scripture for a good five minutes to begin the practice period.
Eleven long out-breaths sounding OM as described on page 95.
Meditate on a text, finally summing up the meaning in OM, for twenty minutes (page 97).
Chant OM for thirty minutes, increasing by five minutes every week, up to one hour.
To end the practice, plunge yourself into one of the four feelings of chapter 13, for a short time.

DAILY LIFE PRACTICE:

Read chapter 11 – independence, perform one of the practices given there.

Read chapter 13 – for relations with others.

Regularly read verse 14 on page 74 and try to cultivate one of the qualities each week.

At the end of six weeks, when the practices are becoming established, read the whole book.

Part One

The Text

1. Śaṅkara in the 8th century A.D. founded four main monasteries, one in each of the four corners of India. The chief is at Śṛingeri in the south. The late HH Abhinava Vidyātīrtha was the thirty-fifth head in unbroken succession from the founder.

1. The Sacred Texts

The Vedas are sacred revelations to the Aryans of India, some of them at least 5,000 years old and traditionally much more. They contain hymns to gods and to the universal spirit, prayers and sacrifices for the individual's success and happiness in this world and the next, ethical instructions like 'speak the truth' and 'let an uninvited guest be a god to you'. All these are directed to the human being as an individual. This is the first path of the Vedas.

But there are other texts which give instructions on how to leap out of individuality altogether and be one with the universal spirit which is beyond even the gods. This is the second of the 'two paths', and with it the present text is concerned. They are 'paths' – concerned with effecting a change, not merely dogmas to be fanatically clung to. Knowledge of facts for their own sake has never been valued in Indian thinking; it was thought as pointless as the compulsive counting of leaves on a tree. Knowledge was prized for its results. The holy texts were not concerned with philosophical speculations indulged in by people who did not want to move; they were directions to a path for those who wanted to go along it. The two paths lead, respectively, to happiness, success and blessedness for those who want to remain individuals in this world and the next; and second, to throwing off individuality and becoming one with universal consciousness for those who feel individuality, even in heaven, as an imprisonment.

The Vedas include both paths. The instructions on freedom, the second path, come mostly in the texts called Upanishads or private instructions, which come at the end of the Vedas. They came to be called Vedanta (Veda-anta, 'end of the Veda'), and as such are sometimes contrasted with the much more numerous texts concerned with the first path. In the Gita, for instance, the Lord says, 'It is I who am to be known by all the Vedas, I am indeed the author of the Vedanta as well as the knower of the Vedas.' Here it is being said that the divine Knower of the Vedas extracted the texts of the second path to make the Vedanta, or Upanishads. In fact the full title of the Gita is 'the Upanishads sung (gita) by the Lord'.

The instructions include information about facts in this world, but this is subsidiary to the main teaching of the path. For instance, texts of the first path require worship of gods who keep in order the processes of nature, which otherwise would be in chaos. Much of the physical clumsiness and emotional frustration of sceptical city-dwellers arises from the loss of reverence for the things and processes of nature; there is no unity of self, technically called tad-atmyata, between the man and what he sees and handles. Descriptions of the gods are given, to help the act of worship. The great teacher Shankara, commenting on these passages, says that the descriptions are true, but they are not the main purpose of the texts, so they are not to be taken as complete, nor argued over.

Again, a very old text (Aitareya Brahmana) remarks that the sun never sets nor rises; it is simply that people think he sets and rises. Shankara says of this sort of statement that though it is true, it is only incidental to the purpose of the Veda. Details about the order of creation, given in varying forms in the Upanishads, are reconciled with one another by Shankara at considerable length, but he emphasises that the texts are not seeking to give exact accounts of the process. What they all declare is that it is conscious and purposeful, arising from one supreme reality called Brahman or universal Self.

Texts must not be relied on for purposes other than what they exist for. It is interesting to read in the royal household accounts that King John bathed three times in 1212, paying only eight-pence to the ewerer or water-carrier who prepared the baths; such facts throw light on life in the early thirteenth century. But to expect to extract an account of social life in the Middle Ages merely from these household accounts would be ridiculous; that was not their purpose. Great areas of social life would not be touched in them.

The Nobel prize-winner J.C. Bose remarked that it was having heard in childhood the Upanishadic statements that there is consciousness in everything, which gave him the impulse to investigate reactions in plants; the Japanese physicist Hideki Yukawa, also a Nobel prize-winner, has said that the ancient Chinese classic Tao Teh King was a great influence on his ideas. But it would be wrong to analyse these revelations in the hope of scientific statements about biology or physics; to give that is not their purpose. They may provide hints, but they are not textbooks of science. There is a tradition that we have today only about one twentieth of the original Vedic corpus. Quoting a text, 'infinite are the Vedas', Dr Shastri told his pupils that the revelations transmitted by the great spiritual lights in all religions are properly called 'Vedic'.

Texts of the second path also give some information about things of this world – for instance that in the natural course of events, man passes from waking, first into a state of dream and then into deep sleep, returning from that through the dream-state. It is also stated that individual man can meet the gods face to face, in this life. Here too the information given is subservient to the aim of the path, which is to transcend individuality altogether.

The inspirations are transmitted through human beings, though they are not taken to originate from merely human experience; they must however be practised and finally verified in experience. The commentary on the Chapter of the Self remarks that it is not a question of a viewpoint created merely by accepting the words of revelation; one must be able actually to take his stand on them. A viewpoint is one thing, and a standpoint is another; it is a basis for action as well as vision.

The Vedic revelations have been heard from those who speak from actual experience; they are therefore called 'heard' (shruti), and are also called 'direct experience' by Manu, himself one of the Vedic sages. There is another body of texts which Manu calls 'inference', and are called by others 'remembered' (smriti); these texts select Vedic passages and systematise and draw conclusions from them. In this translation they are called 'tradition'. Tradition too is authoritative, but it is thought that certain traditions are more applicable to some eras than to others; Dr Shastri said, for instance, that the Bhagavad Gita, which is a tradition, is especially suitable to the present age. It makes the Upanishads easier to understand and practise for all classes of men, whereas some parts of the original Upanishads are extremely difficult.

The Chapter of the Self comes from the Law-book of Apastamba, which is a tradition. In this chapter the Law-book quotes verses from an Upanishadic source which we do not now possess. For the historical details and the parallels with a known Upanishad, the Katha, see Dr Nakamura's analysis translated in Appendix 1. As he says, the Apastamba, in about 500 B.C., is perhaps the first text known to us in which there is this purposeful selection of texts of revelation to express the Vedanta in clear terms. This does not mean that it was not being done already in private between teacher and pupil – in fact there are accounts of such instruction in the Upanishads themselves, where a single text is concentrated upon, and deeper and deeper realisations attained through it. But the Apastamba, like the Gita somewhat later, is a published text accessible to all, in which the procedure is clearly demonstrated.

2. The Law-book of Apastamba

The ancient law-books dealt with domestic, social and religious life, including directions for the ruler. Civil and criminal law naturally were a considerable part, but crimes were also offences against the moral law, and there were elaborate instructions for expiation of sins in general, as well as general directions for purification of conduct.

There are six major law-books extant today, and over thirty less important ones; others are known from the fact that they are quoted in later works.

The Apastamba Law-book is thought to be the oldest of them all, dating from 600–500 B.C. in its present form. In this earliest text there is not much about the formal rituals which developed later, and more stress is laid on right personal behaviour. This law-book emphasises faith as the guiding principle of all religious action; it condemns such motives as name and fame, even saying that where these exist, the result of religious action may be a positive loss of merit. Prayers morning and evening, some offering to the gods, to men, and to animals must be practised every day. The offerings to men consist of charity according to one's means.

Many of the rules show considerable human feeling. Whereas some early systems of law tend to assume the guilt of one arrested – why otherwise should he have been taken up? – Apastamba lays it down clearly: 'where there is a doubt, no punishment.' Theft was punished severely, but where a starving man has taken food to save his life, Apastamba lays it down that there is no penalty. In this book there are indications that the position of women and the lower castes was much higher than it later became; this is thought to be a pointer to a very early date, as is the declaration that beef may be eaten.

Like the other law-books, Apastamba's work lays emphasis on the importance of meditation. He indicates that even worldly activities are not completely successful without meditation, and he makes it of supreme importance for the path of liberation, namely knowledge of Self. The later law-books like the famous work of Manu pay the same attention to meditation – 'let him, concentrating his mind, fully recognise in the Self all things, both the real and the unreal.' Apastamba in the Chapter of the Self had said: 'the seer meditating, seeing everything in the Self, will not be deluded; and whoever sees the Self alone in everything, he is Brahman, glorious in the highest heaven.'

That these were not only words is confirmed by the account of the Greek ambassador Megasthenes, who lived in India in around 300 B.C., not too long after the composition of the Law-book of Apastamba. He says that the philosophers in India practise endurance, and will remain a whole day in one posture without moving. Megasthenes, who was a historian, would have been familiar with something similar in the life of Socrates, who is described as sometimes passing into a state of meditation during which he did not move for long periods. There was even a tradition that Socrates came into touch with Indian thinkers; a fragment is preserved by the historian Aristocles, and later by Eusebius, who gives an account of how an Indian met Socrates in Athens and asked him what was the character of his philosophy. When Socrates replied that it was an investigation into human life, the Indian laughed and said, 'You cannot fix your gaze on human truth without a knowledge of the divine.'

3. The Chapter of the Self

This chapter comes in the part of the Apastamba Law-book concerned with atonement for sins committed. The doctrine of karma (literally 'action') was that the consequences of an action extend into the moral and psychological realms, according to a law of cause and effect, as fixed and predictable as that in the physical realm. Actions prescribed by the holy texts as good will lead to happiness and favourable circumstances in this and future lives; actions condemned as bad will lead to suffering and adverse circumstances.

The acts prescribed as good are what is called dharma or duty, and dharma varies according to the situation of an individual. For instance a king who has the duty of protecting his subjects against invasion cannot practise the pacifism (a-hinsa) which is part of the dharma of a wandering monk; the king sees the world as consisting of separate entities, and he discharges his responsibility to those of them whom he has undertaken to protect, by diplomacy and where necessary by fighting. The wandering monk is one who has seen the Self in everything and everything in the Self, and his duty is calmness of mind and senses, endurance, standing back from the world, faith and meditation (samadhi). This karma, says Shankara in his great commentary on the Brahma-sutras, is simply a reinforcement of his Self-realisation. There was a view that once an action had been performed, its results were unavoidable and unchangeable, but most of the teachers believed that the effects of some sins at least could be modified by carrying out certain austerities. The famous Law-book of Manu lays stress on repetition with devotion of the sacred syllable Om, praised as an expression of God himself, and also on control of the life currents (prana) by special techniques. Fasting was regarded as effective, and various forms were taught – reducing the mouthfuls from fifteen a day at full moon to one a day at the new moon, and so on. Apastamba recommends prayer and meditation for those who wish to reduce the effect of their faults and increase their merits as individuals, but he introduces a section called the Chapter of the Self, which is for those who wish to follow the second path of the Vedas, namely to get out of individuality and become universal.

He begins by telling the aspirants to practise 'yogas of the Self', later described as practising characteristics like freedom from anger, speaking the truth, sharing with others, nobility, contentment and others. The method is called yoga because the basis is meditation. It was not thought effective to force oneself to perform charity, for example, while inwardly grudging the money, or to show an outward amiability while inwardly seething with anger. Shankara remarks that without meditation practice, such inner feelings cannot be really controlled.

The traditional method of yoga was to meditate on one of these things, in the form of an actual incident, every day; in time the practice reaches what is called samadhi, a meditation state where consciousness of meditator and the act of meditating disappear, and the object alone remains, shining out in a radiant form. When this happens, the roots of the mind have been substantially changed, and the characteristic is becoming natural to the yogi.

The meditations slowly make the mind clear and steady. Opposed to them are what are called doshas. The word dosha is left untranslated here. It comes from a root whose sense is that something has gone wrong, that something natural has been defiled or spoiled or impeded in its operation. The main idea is that something is not what it should be naturally, or is not working as it should work naturally. A flaw in an argument is a dosha, bad light is a dosha to a man who is looking for something (though not to a blind man who is groping for it). A thing is a dosha only in a particular situation. Anger, says the Law-book, is a dosha to a man seeking freedom, because it disturbs his mind and binds him firmly in his individuality; for the first of these reasons, it is also a dosha in the way of worldly success. Though an angry man can often overbear a lazy man, simply because he is more aroused, he will generally lose to an energetic opponent who yet keeps inwardly calm. The angry man always tries to force things, uses unnatural means, and is therefore subject to 'dosha'.

When the yogas are being practised and the mind has been partially steadied, at least sometimes, the yogi is told to practise realisation of the Self. 'Each and every living being is the city belonging to the one lying at rest in the cave, indestructible, taintless, the unmoving abiding in the moving. Those who practise realisation of it, they are immortal.' When an untrained man looks within, he finds, as David Hume did, nothing but a flux of thoughts, feelings and so on, and no enduring self at all. Hume allowed that others might find one, but that was irony. No indestructible, taintless, unmoving self is found. Without skill in meditation, as Shankara says repeatedly in his Gita commentary, the Self is not made out clearly, though it is in fact always being experienced as the support of the inner and outer worlds. But it is not recognised; people believe that these worlds support themselves.

The yogi shakes off the moving thoughts and sensations and feelings and memories as they arise, and looks calmly and steadily *through* them, as it were, to find in the changing flow something which does not change.

The shaking off is not done by force; that would produce further agitation. A modern teacher has remarked that it is something like the way in which sober people shake themselves free from the attentions of a maudlin drunk who is looking for a listener. They simply pay no attention to him. At first he becomes more insistent, but as he presses himself on them they take no interest; they look through him, neither answering nor arguing nor reasoning with him. They keep turning away, so that he has to go round the other side. Drunken men vary in their persistence, but as they have paralysed the higher powers of the mind which can exercise patience, they can never last as long as sober people who are determined to have nothing to do with them. After a time, getting no reaction, the intruder turns away to look for more favourable circumstances. The next day he may be back, but after six weeks, finding that he never gets any response, he gives up.

This is the method of shaking off the doshas at the time of meditation on Self. They can not be shaken off unless they have been already weakened, 'thinned out' as it is said, by the practice of their opposites: calmness, generosity, and so on. That was the meditation given first.

Practice of Self-realisation leads to discovery of something immortal, the undying in the dying. All thoughts and feelings rise and pass away – they are dying. The men in whom they arise are dying. All are dying. But in them, underlying them, is something unchanging which never dies. Even a flash of realisation of this immortal element can free a yogi from the anxieties of a lifetime. But it has to be a real living experience – not an intellectual idea merely.

Two meditations have been described: the meditation on the characteristics like freedom from anger, and the meditation directly on the Self, the undying in the dying. A third meditation is given – on the universal Lord from whom the universe arises, by whom it is supported, into whom it finally returns. This is the universal Self, and the individual Self finally turns out to be the same as that universal Self. The yogi meditates that the objects of the world, and the currents which move them, are from one being; that being has entered everything, and is everything, though in another sense he is beyond everything. The world is meditated upon as the Lord. Under the influence of the doshas, it has been seen as consisting of separate objects impelled by conflicting currents, physical and mental, but if this meditation reaches samadhi, the world is seen and felt as a play of light. Here again, this must be something lived, not simply a notion subscribed to when circumstances are not too overwhelming. The yogi has to feel the universal light as one with the light in himself; when this happens, even briefly, there is a great and lasting effect on mental reactions, and often on the physical plane also.

Here is the basic text, on which Shankara made the commentary which is to be presented later:

The Chapter of the Self
in the Apastamba Law-book (1.8.22 and 1.8.23)

1 Let a man practise in the approved way the yogas of the Self, which make the mind steady.

2 There is nothing higher than attainment of the Self.

3 For that end, we quote some verses which bring about attainment of the Self.

(Now follow verses from some lost Upanishadic source
– Shankara)

4 Each and every living being is the city belonging to the one lying at rest in the cave, indestructible, taintless, the unmoving abiding in the moving. Those who practise realisation of it, they are immortal.

5 This indeed which here in this world and here in that world is called the object –
Having shaken himself free from it, let the seer devote himself to that which lies in the cave.

6 (Pupil) 'Not in the self have I attained it. Now in other things will I seek that place of the good, by detachment.' (Teacher) 'Devote yourself to your welfare, not to your harm. (It is) great, a mass of splendour, all-pervading, the Lord.'

7 He who is constant in all beings, wise, immortal, firm, without limbs, without sound, without body, without touch, great, pure –
He is all, the highest goal, he is in the centre, he divides, he is the city.

8 The yogi who practises realisation of that in everything, and always holds to firmness in that,
Will see that which is hard to see and subtle, and rejoice in heaven.

9 The seer meditating, seeing everything in the Self, will not be deluded,
And whoever sees the Self alone in everything, He is Brahman, glorious in the highest heaven.

10 Subtle, finer than a lotus-fibre, he stands covering all; Greater than the earth, firm, he stands supporting all. He is other than the sense-knowledge of this world. The world is not different from him, who is ever standing as the supreme, who is to be known, who himself divides into many.
From him the bodies all come forth, he is the root, eternal, he is constant.
(This ends the Upanishadic verses)

11 Yoga is the basis for destruction of the doshas here in this life; Having thrown off these which torment beings, the wise one (paṇḍita) attains peace.

12 Now we exemplify the doshas which torment beings:

13 Anger, thrill, irritation, greed, delusion, self-display, spite, false speech, over-eating, back-biting, jealousy, lust and hate, loss of self-possession, absence of yoga. They are shaken off on the basis of yoga.

14 Freedom from anger, freedom from thrill, non-irritation, freedom from greed, being without delusion or self-display or spite, truth-speaking, moderate diet, no back-biting, freedom from jealousy, sharing with others, giving up, straightforwardness, gentleness, calm, control, the yoga which has no

conflict with any being, nobility, kindness, contentment –
these apply to all the stages of life.
Practising them in the approved way, one becomes
all-pervading.

4. Shankara the Teacher

Shankara, the great yogi-philosopher of India who revivified the ancient doctrine of the Upanishads when it was in danger from Buddhist scepticism on the one hand and from the refined materialism of ritualists on the other, is the reputed author of more than 400 works. They can be roughly divided into three classes: commentaries on authoritative texts (there are about 70 of these); about 110 independent treatises which do not follow a text; and some 220 poems, philosophical or devotional. Perhaps a quarter of this great body of works has been translated into English.

It is important to note that Shankara regarded himself as a commentator, and never claimed to be an original thinker as did, for instance, the Buddha. Dr Nakamura's history of early Vedanta has shown that most of the supposed innovations in Shankara's work go back long before him. Shankara claimed to transmit the teaching of the Upanishads concerning Brahman, the ultimate conscious reality who projects, sustains and withdraws this apparent world as an actor projects, maintains and finally withdraws the world of a play. The Upanishads teach that what is felt to be an individual self, imprisoned in body and mind, is fundamentally Brahman, and that this can be realised in experience by first purifying and then transcending the mental preconceptions of individual identity. Shankara's teaching is that by hearing an Upanishadic revelation in reverence, thinking and meditating on it and then transcending mind altogether, it is realised in consciousness. The thinking and meditating are really the consummation of hearing. A cardinal point of his teaching was that it is only from hearing such Upanishadic revelation that liberation is attained; it cannot be attained by unguided mental activity, which leads only to scepticism. Mental activity cannot discover its own basis, any more than arrows drawn on the surface of a paper can point into the paper itself. But a skilled artist can, by using an illusion in the form of perspective, direct attention to depth; and the Upanishadic sentences, though themselves words, can direct awareness beyond words and concepts.

Shankara is generally called Shankara Acharya, Shankara the Teacher. He was also called, especially in the early days, Holy Shankara, Shankara whose feet are holy, Shankara whose holy feet are to be worshipped. He was thus a teacher of sacred things; in one sense of the word, he was not a philosopher at all. Today some philosophers regard their task as clarifying the premisses of activities like science or criminal law. Working on data provided by others (which are, however, often changing), they try to bring out to inspection unexpressed assumptions which underlie words such as 'law' or 'intention'. Using their conclusions, the scientist or lawyer can pursue his business free from irrational prejudices. The philosopher can and should discuss what are the implications, for the theory of knowledge, of the assumption that human language is the basis for discussing something biologically more fundamental, namely the hereditary DNA code. But it is not his business to inquire whether the hereditary code really has generated, of itself, the human speech code; he leaves that to the scientist. In the same way he may discuss what could be meant by a concept of diminished responsibility, but it is not his business to ask how such a doctrine can be implemented in the legal process; that is for the lawyers and social reformers. Shankara's view is quite different. He teaches a system of realisation of new facts, not accessible to any of the normal means of acquiring knowledge, and in the end fundamentally opposed to them. He teaches realisation, which has nothing to do with thinking about the things of the world; also he teaches the means to facilitate and to steady it, and these means do concern activities in the world. The means to facilitate the rise of realisation is called action-yoga or karma-yoga; when Knowledge has arisen, the means to steady it, if necessary, is called Knowledge-yoga or jnana-yoga. Shankara's view of the world, based as it is on the Upanishadic realisations confirmed by him in experience, will never be completely satisfactory to those whose world-view does not include realisation. It will be inconceivable and perhaps nonsensical to them. The situation is well-known in the history of thought. For instance, in 1860 Whewell published his *History of the Inductive Sciences*, in which he actually coined the word 'scientist'. He illustrated the type of scientific progress from the history of two great sciences, astronomy and physical optics. He took as a model of the discovery of truth, the triumph of the wave theory of light over the corpuscular theory (which he calls the emission theory) originally proposed by Newton. Whewell pointed out that there were some residual difficulties in the wave theory, associated with very weak light-sources, but he felt he had strong grounds for dismissing them as purely temporary hold-ups.

Objections were made to the undulatory theory by some English experimenters ... The objections depended partly on the measure of the intensity of light in the different points (a datum which it is very difficult to obtain with accuracy by experiment) and partly on misconceptions of the theory, and I believe there are none of them which would now be insisted on.

He gives an account of the stages of acceptance of a true theory:

We have been desirous of showing that the *type* of this progress in the histories of the two great sciences, Physical Astronomy and Physical Optics, is the same. In both we have many *Laws of Phenomena* detected and accumulated by acute and inventive men; we have *Preludial* guesses which touch the true theory, but which remain for a time imperfect, undeveloped, unconfirmed; finally, we have the *Epoch* when this true theory, clearly apprehended by great philosophical geniuses, is recommended by its fully explaining what it was first meant to explain, and confirmed by its explaining what it was *not* meant to explain. We have then its *Progress* struggling for a little while with adverse prepossessions and difficulties; finally overcoming all these and moving onwards, while its triumphal procession is joined by all the younger and more vigorous men of science.

Here it is assumed, without discussion, that the corpuscular theory of light is opposed to, and exclusive of, a wave theory, and vice versa. Common sense tells us that a stream of particles is quite different from a succession of waves. It *seems* that reason tells us this also, but reason does not inform us about facts, it only organises what is presented to it as fact. Our experience from childhood tells us that waves are different from particles, and their respective behaviours are mutually exclusive; reason carries on from there. Even Whewell's brilliant mind never considered any other possibility, or if he did, he must have dismissed it as ridiculous.

We cannot properly say there ever was an Emission Theory of Light which was the rival of the Undulatory Theory, for while the undulatory theory provided explanations of new classes of phenomena as fast as they arose, and exhibited a consilience of theories in these explanations, the hypothesis of emitted particles required new machinery for every new set of facts, and soon ceased to be capable even of expressing the facts ... the authority of Newton's great name gave [his explanations] a sort of permanent notoriety, and made reflection and refraction ... a standard point of comparison between a supposed Emission Theory and the Undulation Theory. And the way ... they were to be tested was obvious: in the Newtonian theory, the velocity of light is increased by the refracting medium; in the undulatory theory it is diminished. On the former hypothesis the velocity of light in air and in water is as 3 to 4; in the latter as 4 to 3 ...

In 1850 the difficulties were overcome by M. Fizeau and M. Foucault separately; and the result was that the velocity of light was found to be less in water than in air. And thus the Newtonian explanation of refraction, the last remnant of the Emission Theory, was proved to be false.

Thus Whewell concludes by giving the 'crucial experiment' which 'refuted for ever' the corpuscular theory first put forward as a suggestion by the great Newton.

And yet today it is generally believed that light displays the characteristics of either particles or waves, depending on the testing conditions. It is interesting that a decisive demonstration of the existence of light as consisting of particles was the photoelectric effect, associated with the very weak sources of light which Whewell had scrupulously noted as a possible difficulty for the wave theory, though he ultimately dismissed it. We are today forced to accept that light has the properties both of waves and of particles. To a scientist a hundred years ago this would have seemed meaningless, or irrational, by which he would have meant conflicting with experience so far.

Whewell had not the delicate apparatus to experiment with the photo-electric effect. There was no absolutely compelling evidence to make him revise his common-sense view of the mutually exclusive nature of the opposing theories; he had his doubts, but he brushed them aside by a sort of act of faith.

This little episode in the history of science is not mentioned to make us smile at the Victorian scientists; their achievements were very great. It can however make us see that what seem logical absurdities and impossibilities may nevertheless be facts.

In Shankara's teaching, after a certain point, there is a challenge to the ordinary man's most fundamental convictions. These are not unchallengeable facts supported by reason, as he believes, but arise from a confused analysis of experience. Delicate apparatus, namely a clear and concentrated mind in the meditation called samadhi, is necessary to see the true Self. Once seen, it is recognised everywhere.

In Shankara's view, again, the world is partly an illusion, like a show put on by a magician, or the 'world' projected by an actor. Worldly knowledge corresponds to analysing the character of Hamlet or the geography of the play; it has interest and value, but it is not concerned with something absolutely real. It is to be noted that the worlds of Shakespeare's plays have their own history and geography *in* them; no account of their real origin will make sense in terms of the play. Within *Hamlet*, no one has painted the castle at Elsinore; it is an ancient stronghold. Yet, in reality, it was painted a week before the performance. There is no painter and no backcloth in the play – the walls are stone. Shankara says of the various creation accounts in the Upanishads that they are true, but it is pointless to study them because they describe the projection of an illusion. They therefore will not make sense within the terms of the illusion. The one important point is that the illusion is consciously and purposefully projected. To know this fact, not as a theory subscribed to but as living experience, changes the reactions to life. If when watching Gloucester's eyes put out, in *Lear*, it is forgotten that the play is an illusion consciously projected as a form of beauty, it will be a terrible experience, from which it might take a long time to recover. When the play is known to be an illusion, the same pity and terror are experienced, but not as absolutely real. To know that the play is an illusion is not to dismiss it as valueless; it has value, but it is not ultimately real. Its value is that it has been created by a supreme genius and the final purpose is beauty. In the same way Shankara stresses that the illusion of the world-projection is projected by a divine Lord who is the 'friend of all beings'. But this realisation will have to be so complete and steady that it is not disturbed even by a sword-cut, as he says.

The Upanishads on which Shankara commented were nearly all completed at least a thousand years before he was born (about 700 A.D. according to many historians). To interpret them he had to be an expert in the ancient language, and some of the commentaries attributed to him are now thought to be spurious just because they make mistakes in interpreting ancient Sanskrit, mistakes of a kind which the real Shankara does not make in his genuine works.

There were other authoritative works on which he commented which were not Upanishads, though of immense spiritual authority. One of these was the Bhagavad Gita. Some of the others later came to be called Upanishads, though Shankara had not regarded them as such. Productions attributed to Shankara which call such works 'Upanishads' are therefore probably not by him, but written later. Of course this does not mean that they may not be spiritual masterpieces in their own right.

Again, if a work contains references to Tantrik or other ideas which do not appear in the old Upanishads, and which have been found only after Shankara, it is unlikely to be by him. Shankara called himself a follower of the Upanishads and a teacher of Brahman; if some work does not quote even once from the Upanishads, or contains no reference to Brahman in its teaching, it would not be very characteristic of Shankara.

Only eleven of the commentaries on Upanishads by Shankara pass these and the many other critical tests. One more is doubtful – some parts may be by him.

As to other texts, Shankara is believed to have written commentaries on the Brahma-sutra, which was a systematisation of Upanishadic thought, on the Gita, on the Gaudapada verses attached to the Mandukya Upanishad, on the Chapter of the Self in the Apastamba Law-book, and (a recent discovery) on the Yoga Sutras of Patanjali. The rest of the seventy-odd commentaries attributed to him are less well attested, and some are certainly spurious.

Of the 110 independent treatises, the anthology of his verse and prose called 'The Thousand Teachings' is best authenticated, though the greater part of the manuscripts so far analysed omit the prose sections altogether. Perhaps another dozen of the treatises may well be by him, but this leaves nearly a hundred which are doubtful, and some of them must be later than Shankara.

In the same way many of the short philosophical, mystical or devotional poems contain things which Shankara probably would not or could not have written. But the genuine ones have been immensely influential, and some of the others also are masterpieces, though not by Shankara.

In all this it has to be remembered that the present-day critical analysis is based on only the material now available. There may be new discoveries which will upset some of the present assumptions. For example, just over twenty years ago a commentary by Shankara on the Yoga Sutras of Patanjali was discovered which passes all the critical tests. This was a great surprise to scholars who had considered Shankara merely as a philosopher; because they themselves had no confidence in the genuineness of yoga practice, they assumed that Shankara would have had no interest in it either, ignoring the many passages on yoga practice in his Gita commentary. Again, Shankara had access to Upanishads which are no longer extant. In his commentary on Brahma-sutra III.2.18, he quotes, from some Upanishad which he does not name, how Bashkalin asked Bahva to teach him Brahman.

> He asked, 'Teach me, sire,' and the other became silent. When he asked a second and a third time, he replied, 'I do teach you, but you do not realise it. Silent is this Self.'

No such passage appears in any Upanishad which is available today, and the text must have disappeared.

Still more interesting is the case where Shankara gives a commentary on Upanishadic verses whose original had already disappeared by his own time. These verses have been preserved in the Chapter of the Self in the ancient Apastamba Law-book. The Law-book is in prose, but there are verses here and there, and in a number of places some of the verses are expressly stated to have been taken from another source by being introduced by some such phrase as 'Now we quote'. (The editorial 'we' occurs in several places in the Law-book.) The Chapter of the Self, as it is now called, comes in the eighth and ninth sections of the first part. (When considered as a separate work, the sutras are numbered from 1 to 14; in the original the reference is 1.8.22.1-8 and 1.8.23.1-6.)

Shankara says in his commentary that they must come from some Upanishadic source which he cannot or does not identify. But he regards them as important, and in various places in his writings he quotes from the Chapter of the Self. In his Brahma-sutra commentary (2.1.1) he quotes the verse, 'From him the bodies all come forth, he is the root, eternal, he is constant' and in his Thousand Teachings (2.1.38), the verse 'Each and every living being is the city belonging to the one lying at rest in the cave'. Several times in commentaries he quotes the sutra 'Than attainment of the Self, there is nothing higher', and he paraphrases it again and again in the verses of his Thousand Teachings.

The Law-book is now the only source for these texts; Shankara's short commentary on them (which has not to my knowledge been translated before) is one of the few which passes all the tests of authenticity. The doctrine is closely connected with that set out in his Gita commentary, and it will be summarised in the next chapter, before the translation is given.

5. Outline of the Commentary on the Chapter of the Self

First, it is necessary to have a rough idea of certain technical terms:

Self (*Ātman*) universal consciousness, which with human beings is felt to be limited and imprisoned in a particular body or mind. Brahman universal consciousness, generally with reference to its projection, maintenance and withdrawal of this apparent world. Brahman and Ātman are the same.

dosha a defect, something clouding or impeding or spoiling the existence or proper functioning of a thing. In spiritual matters, doshas are states such as anger, hatred, unwillingness to share, absence of meditation, and above all Ignorance – feeling the Self as imprisoned and of special qualities. They are based on false notions.

yoga meditation in a sitting position, and the preservation and exercise of the insights attained during the sitting period, when actively dealing with affairs in the world. Yoga is based on right Knowledge.

Ignorance (*avidyā* or *ajñāna*) Shankara's description of Ignorance, in verse 8, is: taking the Self as conforming to its 'apparent conditioning adjuncts' (*upādhi*). Individually, this is experiencing the Self as just the aggregate of body, senses and mind; cosmically it is to take the universe as a totality of matter energised by unconscious forces, without a purpose.

Shankara uses the words avidyā and ajñāna almost indifferently (though there is a statement that avidyā is one of the doshas, and ajñāna is the seed of doshas).

upādhi this is generally translated by the awkward phrase 'apparent conditioning adjunct' – that is, it is not the nature of the thing but attributed to it by juxtaposition. The reputation of King Edward I for integrity rests on the fact that a Latin phrase 'promised is done' was written on his tomb at Westminster Abbey centuries after his death in quite another connection. But because of the juxtaposition, it was taken to apply to the King (whom his contemporaries thought a rather devious statesman); this is an example of an upādhi.

Knowledge (*vidyā* or *jñāna*) In this text, Knowledge means clear awareness that the universe is an illusory projection from Brahman or the universal Self, and that the human self is really universal, its apparent limitations being part of the illusion; Ignorance (*avidyā* or not-Knowledge) is taking the universe and its divisions as absolutely real. Neither Knowledge nor Ignorance refer to an intellectual posture; they are direct experiences. Shankara occasionally here uses the word 'direct-vision' (*saṃyag-darśana* – a favourite phrase of his, occurring frequently in the Yoga-sutra commentary) as a synonym of knowledge.

saṃsāra life as an individual, dying and being born in life after life, always accompanied by suffering because of the frustration of the freedom which is obscurely felt to be natural. Saṃsāra is an endless circle of (1) Ignorance and other doshas, which give rise to (2) activity, which gives rise to (3) ideas of what should be done and what should not, which produce (4) intentional action as an individual (karma), which as its result throws up (1) doshas again.

karma literally 'action', but including the results of action also in the moral and psychological fields, causing experiences of pleasure and pain, circumstances favourable or unfavourable in this and future lives.

As action, karma means an intended operation by an agent, i.e. a man who thinks 'I am acting'. An involuntary cough would not be an action in this sense, but if a cough were to give a signal or express disapproval, it would be.

To the spiritual aspirant of the Law-book, action is perfected when it is fulfilling of the duties (dharma) prescribed for his particular station of life, accompanied by the proper religious attitude as expressed in rituals and sacrifices, and without a selfish desire for the results (though favourable results must inevitably follow).

guṇa is often translated 'quality of nature' or 'aspect'. There are three: *tamas*, which is born of Ignorance as the *Gītā* says, and is inertia leading to darkness; *rajas* is passion-struggle, giving energy and attachment to action. These two correspond to the Yin-yang of the Chinese philosophical school. But in the Indian tradition there is one more, *sattva*, which is clarity and the harmony of health. It produces happiness and knowledge in a possessor, but also binds him by attachment to happiness and to knowledge, if that remains merely intellectual.

It is customary for a commentary to begin with a statement of what the text is about, what is its purpose, and for whom it is intended. The Law-book has been concerned with a man who feels himself to be an agent; this man wishes to wipe out, or at least lessen, the bad karma he has performed, so he is given penances to perform, which may involve giving in charity, fasting, and devotional practices. Then the Chapter of the Self is introduced for a man who wishes to go beyond individuality altogether; even the pleasures of a heaven no longer attract him, because he knows that they will be only transitory, and will still involve limitation to an individuality.

Shankara's method of exposition, here and elsewhere, is to present a statement from a holy text and then propose various objections to it, which he meets partly by citing other texts, or (in the case of objections raised from a basis of scepticism) by showing that the objection rests on an irrational standpoint. In this way the meaning and implications of the text are brought out more fully. All these objections will rise at some time in some form in the mind of a pupil, and he is shown how to meet them intellectually, against the time when he will have to meet them out of his living experience.

The discussion in the introductory part of the commentary turns on what is meant by action. The objector says that a man is always acting, and that he is directed by the texts to act in accordance with duty (dharma) and avoid sin (a-dharma). Even when a man seeks freedom, he must still continue to engage his consciousness in these actions, thinking 'Here I am, so-and-so, and now I will do this and I shall get that result.'

Shankara's reply is that it is just this conviction 'I am so-and-so, and now I will do this' which is the cause of imprisonment in a body. If he wants freedom he should give up this conviction and feel 'I am the universal spirit'. The objector replies, 'The holy texts say that every individual must perform the actions which are his proper duty in his particular situation in life', and Shankara says, 'They do indeed say that, but these directions are given to individuals, to people who feel that they *have* a situation in life. They cannot apply to the universal spirit.'

The point is made again and again in Shankara's writings. It does not mean that when there is no individuality now functioning in that body and mind, they will necessarily cease from working. But what they do will be a direct expression of the universal spirit, and not an impulse from an individual concerned with his own interests, especially the interest of self-preservation.

The doctrine of the original text, and this commentary on it, follows closely the passage in the Brihadaranyaka Upanishad (3.5.1):

> the knower of Brahman, having known that wisdom, should seek to stand on the strength of it; having realised wisdom and strength, he meditates in silence; having realised silence and non-silence, he is a knower of Brahman. How should he behave? However he should behave, he is just that. Except this, everything is perishable.

He is a knower of Brahman at the beginning as at the end; the 'strength' and 'meditation' are simply throwing off attachments which try to revive and hold him to an individuality in the world. Shankara in his commentary on this Upanishad remarks that it would be expected that one on the path of yoga of knowledge, which begins with knowledge of Self, would become a renunciate, but 'however he should behave, he is just that'. Shankara adds that the behaviour will not be meaningless, and he himself, though he became a monk, founded monasteries which flourish today, and transformed the whole spiritual climate of India. All the voluminous commentaries on the Upanishads and the Gita which came before him were superseded by his own, terse but profound.

These are the main points of the discussion in the introduction.

In verse 3, Shankara points out that just practising yoga, meditation sitting, without a penetration into the true nature of the Self, does give temporary calm and clarity. But it cannot last, because the consciousness of individuality, though temporarily forgotten, springs up again in a man who has not pierced through to the nature of what he really is. So there is no freedom. Therefore there must also be an acceptance of some Upanishadic revelation, not simply intellectually but in the depths of the being.

Then verses 4 and 5 give a method of penetrating to the Self. Self is concealed behind the thoughts and emotions, and beyond them, by the buddhi, the spiritual peak of the mind, which is yet a veil. The Self is said to be at rest in a cave. Often a cave in a hillside in India is not apparent; it is not clear that there is a cave there at all. The cave has to be located. In the midst of the shifting senses and mind and buddhi, the yogi has to search very carefully and calmly, to find the hidden place where there is something which does not move – the unmoving concealed in the moving, the undying in the dying, light concealed by darkness, universality imprisoned in a dream. In verse 6 the pupil says that he has not been able to find it within himself: surely God must be outside. The teacher says that God is indeed outside, but it must not be thought that He is not in one's own Self. The teacher describes for the pupil forms of meditation on the Self as universal, especially in terms of light and splendour. These meditations are not simply thoughts, beginning and ending as ideas in the mind. They have to be carried to the point where experience changes, where there is a direct vision of the Lord as the universe, as given in the Eleventh Chapter of the Gita. It may be noted that there Arjuna, the pupil, was overwhelmed by the vision, as Saul was overwhelmed on the road to Damascus. The descriptions are not poetic similes.

In verses 7 and 10 there are references to some Upanishadic accounts of the projection of the universe in a particular order of five 'elements'. These are not the earth and fire which we know here, but subtle principles in a realm beyond the human mind. Shankara subscribes to the accounts, and in several of his commentaries he carefully reconciles them, but he adds that discussion of the details has no importance for spiritual progress; the one point which is really important is that beyond them all, and consciously projecting them, is a Lord, the universal Self.

In verse 8 Shankara gives one of his rare definitions of Ignorance. It is seeing the Self-nature as conforming to the 'apparent conditioning adjunct' – thinking that the actor really suffers and dies as Othello, or partially controls his world as Oberon or Prospero.

Here there is the first statement that the realisation is first attained by 'great skill in samadhi meditation', and must afterwards be firm and steady. The word translated 'skill' is used in the commentary on the Patanjali Yoga-sutra several times; it has also the sense of clearness in meditation.

In verse 9 the text makes the same point, that the Self is first seen in meditation. 'The seer meditating, seeing everything in the Self, will not be deluded.' 'Seeing everything in the Self' means with the senses withdrawn, as a tortoise withdraws his limbs. But Shankara points out that the next line, 'seeing the Self in everything', means that the yogi can and must retain the insight of the meditation when the body is going about and dealing with the world. This means that the mental layers have become so thinned that the universal Self shines clearly through them, although the objects of the world still register on the senses and thence in the mind. Verse 11 makes one of the main points of the commentary. The man who has seen the Self continues formal yoga meditation, if the remnant of his past karma comes to disturb the mind so that it tends to perpetuate the sense of individuality, though now known to be illusory. The objector makes the apparently very strong point that this must be self-contradictory: either Knowledge frees from illusion, or it does not. If it frees from illusion, no yoga practice would have any meaning, for it would itself be illusion. If Knowledge does not free from illusion the whole notion of a yoga of Knowledge falls to the ground.

The answer is, that the yoga practice is illusory like the rest of the world, but it supports Knowledge because it drives towards universality, rejecting the apparent separations of the world. 'The world is not different from him, who is ever standing as the supreme ... who himself divides into many. From him the bodies all come forth, he is their root, eternal.' The yogas, says Shankara, are associated with right Knowledge, and therefore they are powerful, whereas the doshas, which are founded on false notions, are ultimately weak. They are weak because they are unstable, as an illusion is always fundamentally unstable. In the world the test of an illusion is that it cannot maintain itself.

The disturbances which may arise after Knowledge has appeared are caused by past impressions which continue to operate for a little, though with ever-diminishing force, like a flying arrow. These are the remnants of the karma which has set up the present life; the rest of the karmas are discarded like throwing a quiver of arrows on to the ground without shooting them at all. There may be none of the past impressions left – for instance if the moment of Knowledge is at the very end of life. But it is common that some of them do continue to work themselves out, and they prompt the yogi to action. As there is no individual motivation in the yogi, he does not act from any personal basis any more, and no new karma is created. The past karma dies away like a bell which has been struck and vibrates for some time.

In general these are cases, as Shankara hints in his Gita commentary, where a man has undertaken many responsibilities in the world before his Knowledge arises; the promises made have their own urgency, and after Knowledge his mind and body will be pulled by the undertakings entered into, and will fulfil them, experiencing pleasure and suffering in the process. But these feelings do not press on the awareness of the universal Self which is clear behind them, shining through them as it were. The actions are inspired by the cosmic urges and express the yogas of universal benevolence and so on, set out in verse 14. It is doshas which produce action by an individual, based on Ignorance. The yogas are action expressive of the Knowledge of the universal, and convey the message of the universal spirit to the people of the world. Such action is spiritual teaching, whether the body-mind aggregate is inspired to take that role formally or not. The remainder of these lives is sometimes quite obscure, but they bring a sort of freshness to the people who come into touch with them.

6. Quotations in Śaṅkara's Commentary

Abbreviation	No. of citations	Work cited
Āpas.	9	Law-book of Āpastamba (in prose)
Bṛihad.	7	Bṛihadāraṇyaka Upanishad
Chānd.	3	Chāndogya Upanishad
Gautama	1	Law-book of Gautama (prose)
Gītā	3	Bhagavad Gītā
Iśā	1	Iśā Upanishad
Kāṭhaka	6	Kaṭha Upanishad
Mahābh.	7	Mahābhārata epic
Mahānār.	3	Mahānārāyana Upanishad
Manu	3	Law-book of Manu (in verse)
Muṇḍ.	6	Muṇḍaka Upanishad
Śvetāś.	1	Śvetāśvatara Upanishad
Taitt.	6	Taittirīya Upanishad
Taitt. Ār.	1	Taittirīya Āraṇyaka
Taitt. Br.	1	Taittirīya Brāhmana
Taitt. Sa.	1	Taittirīya Saṃhitā
Unidentified ('ākāśavat sarva-gataśca nityaḥ')	1	Perhaps a lost Upanishadic text

The relative frequency of the quotations from the Upanishads is close to that found in other commentaries of Śaṅkara which are well authenticated.

The citations from non-Upanishadic authority are all found in his other commentaries; the numbers here, though small, show Śaṅkara's usual reliance on the Gītā and the Mokshadharma section of the Mahābhārata epic, and the Law-books of Manu and Āpastamba. As the basic text is a section of the Āpastamba itself, it is natural that there should be here a number of citations of other parts of that book.

7. The Chapter of the Self of the Āpastamba Law-book, with the Commentary of Śaṅkara

1. Let a man practise in the approved way the yogas of the Self, which make the mind steady

Om. Now we begin a concise commentary on the Chapter of the Self, which begins 'Let a man practise in the approved way the yogas of the Self' (adhyātmika-yogās). Why, one may ask, is it brought forward here in a section (of the Law-book) which deals with atonement for sins? The answer is, that both (yoga and atonement) lead to destruction of karma. Atonements lead to the destruction of *undesirable* karma; and to one who sees rightly (vivekin), *all* karma, (even that) prescribed for the various castes and stages of life, is undesirable, because it leads to taking on a body. Knowledge of Self (ātma-jñāna) leads to destruction of karma because it does away with the doshas (defects like anger) which cause activity.

It will be said here that when the wise man (paṇḍita), who knows the Self, throws off the doshas, then both duty (dharma) and its opposite (a-dharma) are destroyed and he attains Peace, and it is to give that Self-knowledge that the Chapter of the Self is begun in this place, the common point being destruction of karma.

Objection But surely the prescribed actions (karma), laid down (by the holy texts) for men in their various castes and stages of life, do not produce results (which would have to be reluctantly lived through by the doer), so it is undesirable to destroy them.

Answer They do, as shown by texts like the one (in this Law-book itself, 2.2.2.3), 'For all the castes, there is supreme and measureless happiness in fulfilling one's own duty (dharma).' And if it be objected that the word 'measureless' must imply attaining Peace (that is, Liberation) – not so, for there are texts like '...there being return to this world because of the effects of karma' (continuation of the same passage). And in the Law-book of Gautama, the text (XI.29) which begins 'They in the castes and stages of life, intent on their own karmas, having experienced after death the results of those karmas...' shows that it is precisely continuance in saṃsāra which is the result of karma.

For in whatever stage of life he may be, a man becomes universal (sarva-gāmin) by practising in the proper way those things which are acknowledged to be destroyers of the doshas, but not by practising some individual duty (dharma). So it will be said (in sūtra 5), 'The seer having shaken off ...' and 'Having renounced truth and falsehood, happiness and pain, the Vedas, this world and the next, let him seek the Self' (Āpas. 2.21.3).

Objection There is the text 'Following all these things as taught, without being distracted, he goes to Peace' (2.21.2), and there the word Peace has the meaning of Liberation. So it is only actions of the various stages of life (performed) *without* Knowledge which have some particular result as their goal, whereas the actions combined *with* Knowledge are means to Peace. Just as poison combined with a mantra, or yoghurt with sugar, produce an effect different (from the usual one – injury or sourness respectively), in the same way here.

Answer Not so. Because attainment of Peace is not something to be *produced*. If it were something to be produced, then indeed there would arise the question whether it would be produced by actions alone, or by actions combined with Knowledge, or by Knowledge and action both, or by pure Knowledge connected with no action. But attainment of Peace is never produced by anything at all, because it is eternal. Therefore it is not correct that actions combined with Knowledge produce attainment of Peace.

Objection (Then let us say that) actions combined with Knowledge are effective – just as much as Knowledge by itself – in *removing the obstacles* to attainment of Peace.

Answer Not so. Because it is just actions that are the obstacles to attainment of Peace, inasmuch as they are causes which have effects. For all actions, arising (as they do) from the dosha which is Ignorance (avidyā), with their effects in the form of happiness and sorrow, are obstacles to Peace. Attainment of Peace is simply freedom from actions, and that freedom is not attained through anything other than Knowledge of Self. So it is said, 'Having shaken off these which torment beings, the wise one goes to Peace' (sūtra 11). 'Wise' here means Self-knowing, for that is the topic. And the holy text says, 'Knowing the bliss of Brahman, he is not afraid of anything' (Taitt. Up. 2.9). For attainment of Peace is fearlessness; another holy text says, 'Fearlessness, O Janaka, you have attained it' (Bṛihad. 4.2.4).

When the teacher (Āpastamba) says, 'Following all these things as taught, without being distracted, he goes to Peace', it is in a different sense. How so? He means that when one carries out the duties of the stages of life so taught, without distraction – without selfish desires – then he becomes qualified for Knowledge; but not when he does as he likes as a desirer of desires, distracted by desires for wife, son, money and so on. The point is this: when he is a Knower (jñānin), then he goes to Peace by the path of renunciation of everything. For no one ever succeeds in throwing off the doshas by means of action. It is just when there is activity (pravṛitti) that we see the doshas with their (associated) false-knowledge (mithyā-jñāna) gaining the ascendency (over the yogas). So tradition says 'Desire has its root in intention' (Manu 2.3). And with slackening of activity, we see that the doshas do become thinned out. Unless these with their false-knowledge have been shaken off, no one attains Peace. Nor could prescribed actions extinguish the *good* karmas accumulated from previous births (even admitting that the bad ones might be so extinguished), because they would not be opposed to each other, both of them being pure. And while good karmas remain, there will still be taking on a body to live through their results, and from that, desire and aversion impelling to duty (dharma) and its opposite, and so again taking on a body. How then would saṃsāra ever be stopped? Therefore, neither attainment of Peace nor removal of the obstacles to it come from actions.

Objection Then let us say that removal of (the root obstacle) Ignorance (avidyā) comes from Knowledge together with actions. Allowing that Knowledge and action are incompatible in that their effects are different, still Knowledge combined with action – just as oil, wick and fire are combined in a lamp – could bring to an end the Ignorance and other doshas which cause saṃsāra.

Answer Not so. There is no attainment of Self without annihilation of action, agent and result, and so combination of Knowledge and action is not possible. In the case of oil, wick and fire in lamps, these things are capable of co-existence and mutual cooperation, so they can join together. But Knowledge and action can never join together because no co-existence and co-operation is possible for them.

Objection The idea of Knowledge alone (as the means) is not right because holy texts are against it.

Answer Not so. Prohibition by (some) texts does not prevent Knowledge having its effect. The conflict is with those texts whose ultimate concern is with how to act; those texts do (it is true) prohibit any total renunciation (saṃnyāsa) even for one following the path of pure Knowledge. But that does not alter the fact that the effect of Knowledge will be to destroy the dosha of Ignorance, as is clear from holy texts like 'the knot of the heart is sundered' (Muṇḍ. 1.2.2.8), 'for him, there is delay only so long' (Chānd. 6.14.2), 'he is freed from the mouth of death' (Kāṭhaka 3.15), and a hundred others from revelation (śruti) and from tradition (smṛiti).

For it is the texts concerned with activity (pravṛitti) that take injunctions to action as above all. And they cannot set aside the essential fact of Knowledge, whose field is the oneness of Brahman and Self. For to do that would be to deny the authority and meaning of all the Upanishads and also traditions like 'each living being is the city' (sūtra 4), 'the Self indeed is all gods' (Manu 12.119) and others.

So although the texts on pure Knowledge, with their field the oneness of the Self, are few, and they are opposed by texts concerned with activity which are many, nevertheless because Knowledge and its effect are stronger, nothing can stand against them.

Objection Knowledge does not invariably bring Peace, for it does not remove the suffering of this present life.

Answer It does bring Peace (as we know) from sacred texts like 'the knot of the heart is sundered' (Muṇḍ. 2.2.8), 'the knower of Brahman attains the highest' (Taitt. 2.1), 'having seen it, he is freed from the mouth of death' (Kāṭhaka 3.15), 'he who knows Brahman becomes Brahman indeed' (Muṇḍ 3.2.9) and from tradition and reasoning (nyāya).

Objection Since it is forbidden by so many texts, the teaching about giving up everything should itself be given up, as in fact people do (give it up).

Answer Not so, for (all) texts are of equal authority. The sacred teaching (Mahānār. 78.12) speaks of all actions (from physical) up to mental, and then says, 'Renunciation (nyāsa) alone excelled these lower austerities (tapas).' Having thus explained actions – here called tapas – as being 'lower', that is, within the field of saṃsāra, this text points to immortality as the result of pure Knowledge, here called renunciation, in these phrases: 'renunciation alone excelled' and 'by giving up (tyāga) some attained immortality' (Mahānār. 12.14). And the text 'for the one who knows this, the sacrificer in his sacrifice is the Self' (Mahānār. 80) and other texts show that for the one who knows, there is no action (karma) at all. And there is another text, 'There are two paths on which the Vedas are based, the first being the path of action and the other being renunciation (saṃnyāsa). Of these two it is renunciation which is higher' (Mahābh. XII.241.6).

Objection Renunciation is not right (yukta) because the texts forbidding it condemn it specifically.

Answer Not so. They are to be taken as intending to praise action for the unenlightened man. Those of dull mind, whose goals are visible things of the world, have to be excited to action by attractive descriptions. (But) the wise do not have anything visible as a goal of action. Condemnation of one thing may be (really for the purpose of) praise of something else, and so in the declarations by teachers condemning pure Knowledge, the main purpose is to praise action.

(It is true that a declaration like) 'If peace has been reached by the wise man, he knows no suffering in the world' (Āpas. 2.21.16) does not decisively declare that Knowledge is to be the means, but this (objection) is to be met with texts like 'the Knower of Brahman attains the highest' (Taitt. 2.1). And other teachers have said, 'give up duty (dharma) and its opposite' (Mahābh. XII.329.40), 'the buddhi does not go there' (XIV. 46.48), 'he is to practise actionlessness (naishkarmya)' (XIV. 46.18), 'therefore they do no action' (XII. 243.7).

So, attainment of Peace is from pure Knowledge alone.

(End of introduction – now the sutras are commented on individually.)

(Let a man practise in the approved way the yogas of the Self, adhyātmika yogās, which make the mind steady.)

adhyātmika yogās Adhyātmika means that they relate to the Self. The shortening of the initial vowel is a Vedic usage. What are the adhyātmika yogas? They will be listed in sūtra 14 as freedom from anger and the others. They are yogas because they bring the mind to samadhi, and they are adhyātmika because they do not depend on external causes. *(Let one practise) those adhyātmika yogas in the approved way*, which means in the established way. For it is when practised in the approved way that the yogas have power to destroy the doshas on the occasion of anger or the others. *which make the mind steady* Anger and the other doshas are disturbing in the sense that they make the indwelling mind go out to sense-objects. Opposed to them are these yogas, which make the mind steady. For at the times of angerlessness and so on, the mind is at peace in its true nature of not running out, and remains at rest on the true Self.

So the yogi should *practise* them, should devote himself to them, which means that he should perform samādhi on freedom from anger and so on. In this way the supreme Self, which is his own Self, is attained. For the Self, though one's own, is not realised as the supreme by a consciousness borne off by doshas like anger, and it is as it were unattained by the people. Therefore let a man practise yoga to attain it.

Objection Everyone knows that attainment of sons and wealth and so on are the highest ends – what could attainment of Self bring?

2. There is nothing higher than attainment of the Self

than attainment of the Self, than perception of the true nature of the supreme Self.

there is nothing higher, no other attainment higher. So in the discussion in the Bṛihadāraṇyaka Upanishad it is said, 'That indeed is dearer than the son' (1.4.8) or than anything else.

3. For that end we quote some verses which bring about attainment of Self

Though the doshas, anger and the rest, which act as obstacles to attainment of Self, are indeed shaken off by freedom from anger and the other yogas, yet they are not quite extinct. For the root sprouts again, since Ignorance (ajñāna) which is the seed of all the doshas, has not been extinguished.

And in that case, their seed not being annihilated, anger and the rest though extinguished for the time will spring up again and there will be no final cutting off of saṃsāra. There is no extinction of Ignorance (ajñāna), which is the seed of those doshas, except by Knowledge (jñāna), and here there are quoted some verses from some Upanishad(s) of other Vedic schools, chosen to give knowledge of Self, which means illumination of its nature.

For that end – the word is literally 'there', but the locative has the sense of 'aim'. So it means, with the aim of attaining the Self.

We quote: select and bring forward

verses which bring about attainment of Self which have the power to make the Self attained as clearly as if set on the palm of the hand. The meaning is, that the verses are strung together in what follows.

4. Each and every living being is the city belonging to the one lying at rest in the cave, indestructible, taintless, the unmoving abiding in the moving. Those who practise realisation of it, they are immortal

the city the city of the body.

living being one that has life.

Each and every living being, from the first-born god down to a tuft of grass, is as it were the city. And a city is the place to find its king. To whom does the city *belong*? To the Self, at rest in the cave. Just as the king is to be seen, surrounded by ministers and others, in his city, so in the bodies is the Self found, associated with buddhi and other faculties. And he sees experiences presented to him by buddhi and the others. He is said to be *the one lying at rest in the cave* because he lies in the cave of buddhi which has become a very veil of Ignorance. His is the city. In that buddhi, when the impurity of Ignorance (avidyā) and the other dash as is removed, he is seen by the knowers who have given up their feverish desires.

There is a further description of the one lying in the cave. *Indestructible*: in the body struck down by a cut or thrust, by age or disease, he is not struck down. In the Chāndogya Upanishad it is said, 'By the killing of this, he is not struck down' (8.10.4). Then he is said to be *taintless*. There is no taint, no sin, in him. For all action whether it may be called righteous or unrighteous, accompanied by the dosha of Ignorance becomes a taint, and it is denied of him by the word 'taintless'. The effects of such action, effects like the pains of age, illness and so on, have (already) been denied by the word 'indestructible'.

Thus every living being is the city, the place where is found the one free from the relations of cause and effect, who is not a saṃsārin (prisoner in saṃsāra). Nor is there any other to be a saṃsārin. For the Śvetāśvatara Upanishad says, 'One god hidden in all beings' (6.11), and the Kāṭhaka Upanishad, 'This Self hidden in all the beings does not shine forth' (3.12); the Upanishad of the Vājasaneyins says 'there is no other seer but this' (Bṛihad.

5.8.11), and the Chāndogya 'That is the Self; that thou art' (6.8.7).

In the first part of the verse, Brahman has been spoken of as it really is; the latter half will speak of the result of realisation for the one who realises it. That indestructible and taintless one, of whom each and every living being is the city, must evidently be all-pervading like space, inasmuch as every being is associated with him. And the holy text says 'Like space, all-pervading and eternal' (unidentified).

Again, it is evident that something all-pervading will be unmoving. That *unmoving abiding in the moving* is itself lying within the moving mind of the living being, and thus is the unmoving abiding in the moving.

Those who practise realisation of it, who attain it directly as 'my own Self', *they are immortal*, immortality is their nature.

How is that devotion to be done?

5. This indeed which here in this world and here in that world is called the object – Having shaken himself free from it, let the seer devote himself to that which lies in the cave

This which is directly experienced by perception: pleasures of women, food, drink and so on. The particle *id* (indeed) has the (distributive) force of 'anything' – this which is perceived whatever it may be.

here means in this world.

the object the exceptional neuter form in the Sanskrit of the word may be taken either from attraction to the earlier (neuter) word 'this', or as a mere shift of gender, or as some Vedic usage, or it may be that the word is capable of both genders.

The word *id* (indeed) and the word *iha* (here) are each repeated, and this must have significance. The second *id* is thus to be taken in the sense of 'and', and the second *iha* means 'in that world'.

The word *world* – like the traditional crow which can look both ways with a single eye – has regard to both *ihas*, so the sense is: *here in this world and here in that world, all this which is called the object.* One standing near or within a heavenly or other world refers to it as 'here in the world' and 'in the world'. *Having shaken free* having rejected all that.

the seer one of transcendental vision, the man of intelligence. Having shaken off ends and means, having come out from the three-fold desire, *let him devote himself to that which lies in the cave*, to the truth of Self thus described.

Where then is that (realisation) to be practised? The verse says:

6. (Pupil) 'Not in the self have I attained it. Now in other things will I seek that place of the good, by detachment.'

(Teacher) 'Devote yourself to your welfare, not to your harm. (It is) great, a mass of splendour, all-pervading, the Lord.'

in the self The form *'ātman'* is a (Vedic) locative. 'In the self' means that the interior self within is the supreme Self, and everything is to be practised as *here*. If it were practised as elsewhere than the body, it would be conceived as not the self. Therefore it is in one's self, in this aggregate of body and senses and mind, having shaken off attachment to outer things, that one should practise realisation of that which lies in the cave, the reality of Self.

Does the sage mean that realisation of it is not to be practised in other things? At the beginning, certainly, realisation of the Self-reality is not to be practised in other things. How then? If in spite of all efforts he does not attain within the body-mind aggregate that Self-reality already described, then the pupil says, '*Now I shall seek* I shall pursue (it) *in other things* like the (divinity in the) sun, *that place of the good*, the place for realising the good, the supreme Self, the place where realisation of the Brahman-reality lying in the cave may be practised, *by detachment*, by desirelessness, after cutting myself away from the pleasures of son, wealth and position.' For practice of Self-realisation and desire for external objects cannot go together.

Well, why should one disregard the many other forms of benefit and practise so hard at Self-realisation alone? The teacher says (to him): '(Those) other things which are not to one's benefit are grasped at under the impression that they are so. But it is different with devotion to Self. How so? Because that is benefit itself. Therefore *devote yourself* to it.'

How is that Self distinguished to which one is to be devoted? The reply is: *great*, of immeasurable extent, because it has neither within nor without, it is the great Self. Such is the greatness of it. Or again, it is great as having guṇas (attributes) as its associated adjuncts (upādhi); it bodies forth, so to say, all things.

a mass of splendour a body of splendour, being in essence the light of supreme consciousness. For it is the splendour of splendours. The holy texts say, 'by whose splendour the blazing sun burns' (Taitt. Br. 3.12.9.7) and 'by his glory all this shines' (Muṇḍ. 2.2.10).

all-pervading in *all* bodies from the first-born god down to a tuft of grass, *pervading*, abiding in them, manifest as essential awareness. Brahman is said to be in the things only in the sense

that they are each a manifestation of Brahman; Brahman has no (actual) location, for it is all-pervading.
the lord he is supreme over all lords, for he is of unthinkable power.

Devote yourself to the Self which is distinguished by an infinity of attributes like these.

7. He who is constant in all beings, wise, immortal, firm, without limbs, without sound, without body, without touch, great, pure –
He is all, the highest goal, he is in the centre, he divides, he is the city.

The injunction to devote oneself to the Self now being described is to be carried over to this verse as well. *He who is constant* undecaying *in all beings* from the first-born god down, who are passing, *wise* intelligent in the sense of omniscient. And thereby

immortal for what is passing and limited in knowledge is found to be mortal, but this which is the opposite of those is immortal.

firm unwavering, of inherently unshaken being;

without limbs the meaning is, without a physical body, for it is in a physical body that head and other limbs exist;

without body that is, without a subtle body (liṅga-śarīra);

without sound there is no attribute of sound in him, for he is the knower of sound, and in the other case (if he himself had the attribute of sound) then it would be (the irrational situation of) what is itself sound cognising what is sound. This cannot be, so he is without sound.

In the same way *without touch*: by the negation of attributes (guṇa) of the two elements Space (ākāśa – locus of sound) and Air (vāyu – locus of sound and touch), negations of all the elemental attributes (bhūta-guṇa) from sound down to odour are to be understood.

Because *great*, it is *pure*, without disguise. The word pure has also the sense of purifier, for a thing which is itself pure is always found to be a purifier, as for instance wind or fire.

And what has been described as the Self, *He is all*, for the Upanishad of the Vājasaneyins says, 'this all is what is this Self' (Bṛihad. 4.5.7). Nothing can be described as apart from the Self, and therefore it is the *highest* supreme *goal*, or limit. 'That is the goal, that is the highest path' says the Kāṭhaka Upanishad (3.11). The meaning is, that of all the paths of saṃsāra this is the end, the consummation, the perfection. *he is in the centre*, in the middle of everything, for the holy text says 'within all' (Bṛihad. 3.16). Again (it can mean) that it is always praised in the mantras to be recited by day at the equinoxes. *He*, the supreme Self.

Objection It has been said that he is all, the supreme goal, and in the centre. Why is it now said that Self-reality is seen as divided?
Answer To this the verse says, '*He* the supreme Self *divides*'. Division is separating out, and in that body where the Self is made out as distinct, there is a 'dividing' – that is the sense of divide. For the body is the place where one becomes aware of the Self as distinct, and Self is thus divided in many ways. As it conforms to the adjuncts (upādhi), divided in every way, none sees it in its purity, but it is seen divided and contrary (to its nature).

8. The yogi who practises realisation of that in everything, and always holds to firmness in that,
Will see that which is hard to see and subtle, and rejoice in heaven.

So the view of one's Self-nature as adapting to its conditioning adjuncts (upādhi), is what is called Ignorance (avidyā). Having removed that by means of Knowledge (vidyā), the view which arises from (studying) the holy texts, let him practise realisation of the Self as thus described. *Always*, in every moment.

Moreover, it is not simply practising realisation – (there must be) *firmness*, a binding to it, a steady consciousness of the delight (rasa) of oneness of the Self, which (consciousness) is of the nature of turning away from quest for external things, and renunciation (saṃnyāsa) of everything. For that is the binding of the Knower to Brahman. Thus bound to Brahman, he does not turn again to the world (saṃsāra). And therefore let him ever hold to firmness in it.

What becomes of the one who is holding to firmness of practice? The verse says,

hard to see it is called hard to see because it is seen with difficulty, through renunciation of fever of desire and so on.

subtle inasmuch as it is hard to see, it is subtle.

the yogin who ... will see that, will directly perceive it, by great skill in samādhi, as 'I am the Self', will *rejoice*. Having seen it thus, he attains the thrill of joy.

in heaven in this Brahman where all sufferings have ceased.

9. The seer meditating, seeing everything in the Self, will not be deluded,
And whoever sees the Self alone in everything,
He is Brahman, glorious in the highest heaven.

The word ātman is (an abbreviated locative) – 'in the Self'. Moreover, *seeing*, perceiving, *everything*, every thing. The meaning is that he is seeing only the Self-nature of every thing, and in everything the Self supreme.

he will not be deluded he does not come to be deluded, for there is no falling into delusion for one who sees the unity of the Self, as witness the Vedic verse, 'There what delusion ...' (Īsā 7). What exactly is this vision of Self which destroys delusion? The verse says, *meditating*, with his senses withdrawn, being a *seer* (kavi), a wise man (medhāvin) in meditation (dhyāna).

Delusion (moha) does not disappear simply by a view (darśana) arising (merely) out of words.

For he who at the time of dealing with the world, keeps restrained-in-yoga (yukta), and sees the one who has entered into all things, *he* indeed *is Brahman*, a man of Brahman, *in the highest heaven* at the zenith in Brahman.

glorious shining forth in many ways.

10. Subtle, finer than a lotus-fibre, he stands covering all; Greater than the earth, firm, he stands supporting all.
He is other than the sense-knowledge of this world.
The world is not different from him, who is ever standing as the supreme, who is to be known, who himself divides into many.

From him the bodies all come forth, he is the root, eternal, he is constant.

And *subtle* all-knowing.

finer than a lotus-fibre more fine than the filament of a lotus.

Who is this? It is that one who is the Self referred to, *covering*, having pervaded, *all* the world.

And then, *greater*, more expanded, more solid, *than the earth*, for he forms the Self of everything.

Firm constant, *supporting* having made the foundation for *all*, for everything, *he stands* he exists. From the indication in the Vedic verse, 'By whom the sky is mighty and the earth firm' (Taitt. Sa. 4.1.8). *He* the lord of all, omniscient, one, who is to be known. He the supreme Self *is other than the sense-knowledge*, than whatever knowledge is produced by the senses, *of this world*; he is described here as different from that worldly knowledge, and from what is said it is clear that he is knowledge itself. 'Existence-knowledge-infinity' says the holy text (Taitt. 2.1.1). So here it is said that he is other than the knowledge about this world produced through the senses. Then it might be supposed that the world is utterly distinct from him, and to rule out that idea, he says, *of this world which is* none other than, *not different from* not separate from *what is to be known* (namely) the highest Lord who is non-dual, the ultimate truth, and who is to be known. He is as it were the clay of which pots and so on are made.

And he is the one *ever standing as supreme* (parame-sth-in). (The word parame-sth-in is explained as:) in his own *supreme* (parame) transcendent glory, *standing* (sth) which means abiding in the space in the heart, and *ever* (suffix -in) – such is he.

Himself alone he *divides*, has separated into gods, ancestors, men and so on, and as the distinction of knower, known and knowledge. So he alone, the Self which is to be known, himself of himself divides the world variously. Thus from the Self alone the *bodies*, the physical frames, *come forth* in order, beginning with space; *all* from the first-born god down. *He* therefore *is the root* of the world, as the holy text says, 'From whom these beings are born' (Taitt. 5.1) and hence he is *eternal*. For whatever is a modification, for instance of earth, will perish in due course as earth dissolves in the (reverse) sequence beginning with water (which had been the preceding element in the order of creation); it will revert to its fundamental cause, and such a thing is not eternal, not constant. And this Self is the ultimate root-cause, there being no further root-cause beyond it. Since what is born will perish, will revert to its ultimate cause, this which is different from those things is therefore eternal, always of the same nature. And it is *constant* because it is one, great, and the ultimate cause. Thus for the man who has known the Self as described, the yogas of the Self (adhyātmika-yogās) practised in the approved way become directly effective. For it is only when preceded by false notions that doshas exist at all. When the doshas cease, samsara also, which arises from them by way of actions of right and wrong, ceases completely. To show this, the verse says,

11. Yoga is the basis for destruction of the doshas here in this life;
Having thrown off these which torment beings, the wise one (paṇḍita) attains Peace.

destruction annihilation, *of the doshas* anger and the rest. The *yogas* are freedom from anger and the others (of sūtra 14).

They are the root, the basis (of practice). For before the yogas, the opposing doshas become weak and can be thrown off. *here in this life* the doshas drive towards remaining (imprisoned) in a body, the point being that life itself is caused by actions (karma) which themselves arise from doshas.

Objection It may be asked, how are those who want freedom to put forth the tremendous efforts in the yogas of angerlessness, etc. which are opposed (to the doshas, the cause of life itself)? Yogas and doshas are mutually exclusive, like movement and rest, and why should it be only the yogas which destroy the doshas, and not the other way round?

Answer To this it is said: The yogas are the strong ones because they are associated with right knowledge (saṃyag-darśana), and the others are destroyed because they are weak, being associated with false notions (mithyā-pratyaya). So it is, that the yogas kill the others, just as in the world it is the men of powerful intellect who destroy the weak-minded. And in this Law-book elsewhere (1.11.25) it is taught that those free from anger are stronger than those subject to anger and passion.

Having thrown off having shaken off, *these which torment beings* when the doshas spring up, beings are scorched by them as if by fire, and so they are called tormentors of beings. Having thrown them off, one goes to Peace, to fearlessness, to freedom. So the holy texts say, 'he who knows the bliss of Brahman is not afraid of anything' (Taitt. 2.9), 'fearlessness, O Janaka – you have attained it!' (Bṛihad. 4.2.4), and the tradition says 'For the Knowers, there is no fear therefrom' (Mahābh. XII. 187. 58).

The verse speaks of the 'wise one' – the paṇḍita. Without knowing Brahman, one does not attain Peace simply by eliminating doshas. For 'paṇḍita' here is used in the sense of knower of Brahman, not knower of doctrine. A holy text about Self-knowledge says, 'therefore the Brahmins, having mastered this wisdom (paṇḍita-hood) ... '(Bṛihad. 3.5.1).

Objection It may be said: if the instruction about shaking off doshas is addressed to the wise man as well, then his Brahman-knowledge has not in fact brought him Peace. If Brahman-knowledge alone brought about Peace, then from the moment of knowing Brahman, he would be free from suffering.

Answer Not so, and this is why: it is just because the yogas are based on the strength of right Knowledge that they have the power to destroy the doshas, which are feeble because they arise from false notions. So attainment of Peace *is* from Knowledge of Brahman, because without that the doshas cannot be eliminated nor karma destroyed.

Objection But then if shaking off the doshas and destruction of karma come automatically from Knowledge, the direction to 'shake off the doshas' becomes superfluous and pointless, because the desired effect will have come about without efforts.

Answer No, because (new) doshas are thrown up by that karma which has already begun to operate. In the matter of producing effects, the karmas accumulated over many incarnations are of two kinds: those already in operation, and those not yet operating. Karma-already-in-operation (pravṛitta karma) is karma which throws up doshas so that the agent shall experience its results in the form of pleasure or pain and so on. Without doshas, there would be no possibility of these results; for in this world we never find a case of pleasure or pain coming into operation without some desire or aversion already there. Therefore the doshas, which have been thrown up by karma-already-in-operation in order to produce its results, and which have grown strong from indulgence in them, are to be thrown off with effort; otherwise they will cause activity (pravṛitti) to prevail (over peace). And this is why it is said that their destruction here in this life is on the basis of yoga.

And furthermore one must take note that there are differences in (degree of clarity of) Knowledge, which may be weak or middling or perfect. For even among those who have Knowledge of Brahman, not all have the same attainment of Brahman; for the highest degree of discriminative knowledge (viveka) is found in (only) some of them, and there is the holy text 'He is *highest* among the Brahman-knowers' (Muṇḍ. 3.1.4) and the tradition '*perfect* in right vision' (Manu VI.74).

The instruction about renunciation (tyāga) and detachment (vairāgya) and conquest of the senses has its meaning for those of weaker or middling Brahman-knowledge. As regards the perfect Brahman-knowers, who have attained the goal already, all this (instruction) is only confirmation (anuvāda) – of what has already been accomplished). The Gītā says, 'only when he has seen the supreme does the inner taste (for sense objects) depart from him'(II.59), and the same thing is said in the Gītā passages on the characteristics of those who have transcended the guṇas (qualities of nature, XIV.22–5).

Objection It might be said, in that case even the enlightened one will be born again, because his karma-already-in-operation is generating doshas which in turn cause activities.

Answer Not so. Because the doshas and (resulting) activities (ceṣṭa) of the Knower have been thrown up (only) by karma-already-in-operation, and their force is being attenuated – as in the case of a shot arrow – just by living through the effects. And since he has no further purposes (to fulfil), there is nothing that could cause another birth. As for the karma which has not already begun to operate, that is burnt in its latent state by the fire of Brahman-knowledge, and like seeds which have been roasted it has no power to germinate into another birth. The holy text says, 'his karmas are destroyed' (Muṇḍ. 2.2.8) and the tradition 'the fire of knowledge burns up all karmas' (Gītā IV. 57).

So the settled conclusion is, that after shaking off the doshas, the wise one attains Peace.

12. Now we exemplify the doshas which torment beings:

13. Anger, thrill, irritation, greed, delusion, self-display, spite, false speech, over-eating, back-biting, jealousy, lust and hate, loss of self-possession, absence of yoga.

Anger is the disturbance of the mind when beaten or shouted at and so on, and it is shown by trembling of the limbs and sweating and the like.

thrill is the reverse of that, arising when something longed for is attained, and shown by tears and movement of the hair and similar signs.

irritation is the particular mental change when something undesired happens.

greed is coveting the property of others, and refusal to use one's own when the time comes.

delusion (moha) is inability to distinguish what ought to be done and what ought not.

self-display is showing off one's own virtues.

spite is seeking to do what others do not want.

false speech is saying what is not true.

over-eating means beyond the proper measure.

back-biting is secretly pointing out the faults of others,

jealousy is resentment at their good points

lust is desire for unlawful intercourse with women.

hate is the ill-will against those who obstruct one.

loss of self-possession is forgetting oneself.

All these from anger onwards are *absence of yoga*, for there is no samādhi in them and they are a kind of distraction of the mind. They are shaken off on the basis of yoga. Then what are the yogas?

14. Freedom from anger, freedom from thrill, non-irritation, freedom from greed, being without delusion or self-display or spite, truth-speaking, moderate diet, no back-biting, freedom from jealousy, sharing with others, giving up, straightforwardness, gentleness, calm, control, the yoga which has no conflict with any being, nobility, kindness, contentment, – these apply to all stages of life. Practising them in the approved way, one becomes all-pervading.

Freedom from anger, freedom from thrill these and the others are the opposite of those (doshas) which obstruct yoga, and these are yogas because samādhi is made on them.

sharing with others distributing one's own means of livelihood to the needy.

giving up (tyāga) abandoning with all one's strength all desired pleasures present or future, and the means to them.

straightforwardness sincerity, and exercising speech, mind and body in an innocent way without disturbance.

gentleness mildness.

calm pacification of the inner organ (the mind).

control pacification of the exterior organs, the senses.

Now another characteristic of yoga is briefly mentioned: *yoga which has no conflict with any being*, for in conflict there is a cause of pain to beings, and without it there is not. This indeed is yoga which causes no pain to any being.

nobility disposition of the noble, without baseness.

kindness no cruelty.

contentment even when failing to get what should be his, his mind is established in tranquillity just as much as if he had got it.

The pacificism (ahiṃsā) which is having no conflict with any being can be only for a Parivrājaka (wandering renunciate mendicant), but the three, Nobility, Kindness and Contentment, apply to all the stages of life, as do such of the others as are not incompatible (with some particular role of life). This is the force of the word 'iti' ('thus' – which comes after Contentment). And since the word 'iti' indicates a class (of things), when he says '*these are accepted for all the stages of life*', it makes things of the same class as Nobility apply to all the stages of life. It means that they are the common ground, so that it is compulsory to practise them.

these as described,
practising, according to rule,
he becomes all-pervading, universal. After passing through the stage of the appearance of Knowledge, he is free.

Thus ends the commentary on the Chapter of the Self in the Āpastamba Law-book, by holy Lord Śaṅkara, an ācārya who is a Paramaharpsa Parivrājaka and disciple of holy Lord Govinda Pūjyapāda.

Part Two

Practice

2. The temple at Śṛingeri.

8. Outline of Practice

The stages of the path are set out clearly by Shankara many times in his Gita commentary, which is closely followed by his commentary on the Chapter of the Self. (They may very well have been written about the same time, in view of the fact that some unusual citations are quoted in both of them, sometimes even in the same pairs.) In Chapter V verse 12, for instance, he gives the stages as follows:

1 karma-yoga (action-yoga) based on the idea 'I do', which produces
2 purity of the mind, in which arises
3 attainment of Knowledge, 'I am Atman'.
4 Renunciation of all actions.
5 Jnana-yoga (knowledge-yoga), based on 'I am'.
6 Peace (liberation).

Karma-yoga itself is divided into four elements practised together:

(a) worship of the Lord;

(b) performing one's duty without attachment to the fruits of the action;

(c) independence of the pairs of opposites such as heat and cold, pleasure and pain;

(d) practice of samadhi meditation.

The steps of the path will be set out in the following sections from the point of view of practice. A point to remember is that 'attainment of Knowledge' in (3) means a direct vision of Self; it is not simply an intellectual idea. Shankara refers to the stages nearly a hundred times in his commentary, explaining them in more detail. Among the phrases which he uses for 'attainment of Knowledge' are:

right vision (samyag-darshana)
vision of the supreme (paramartha-darshana)
knowledge of Self (atma-jnana)
knower of true nature of Self (atma-tattva-vid)
knower of true nature of supreme reality
(paramartha-tattva-vid)
knower of truth (tattva-vid)

These are not theoretical notions.

9. Worship

The first thing for a student of yoga is to find out what he really worships. There are people who claim to worship nothing, to be sceptical; and they say that all worship is a trammelling of the human spirit and intellect, and that it has done far more harm than good. They believe, or claim to believe, that they themselves are able to face unflinchingly the fact that man is a tiny spark of intelligence, born of chance in a vast uncaring and unconscious universe. They say that they do not worship because worship is simply a projection into adult life of the dependence of the infant.

But worship, as the Gita points out, is of various kinds. A worship in the form of tamas or darkness is a worship of some unknown but menacing power. Two prominent sceptics, who both made furious attacks on Christianity in its organised form, were H.G. Wells and Bertrand Russell. If we look at a book which Wells wrote towards the end of his life, we find that he had an awareness, which he believed was justified by philosophical inquiry, of something which he called the Antagonist. In *Mind at the End of its Tether* (Heinemann, London, 1945) he wrote:

> Our universe is the utmost compass of our minds. It is a closed space-time continuum which ends with the same urge to exist with which it began, now that the unknown power that evoked it has at last turned against it. 'Power', the writer has written, because it is difficult to express this unknowable that has, so to speak, set its face against us. But we cannot deny this menace of the darkness.

'Power' is unsatisfactory. We need to express something entirely outside our 'universe', and 'Power' suggests something *within* that universe and fighting against us. The present writer has experimented with a number of words and phrases and rejected each in turn. 'x' is attractive until one reflects that this implies an equation capable of solution in terms of finite being. 'Cosmic process', 'the Beyond', 'the Unknown', 'the Unknowable', all carry unsound implications. 'The Antagonism' by itself overstresses the idea of positive enmity. But if we fall back on the structure of the Greek tragic drama and think of life as the Protagonist trailing with it the presence of an indifferent chorus and the possibility of fluctuations in its role, we get something to meet our need. 'The Antagonist', then, in that qualified sense, is the term the present writer will employ to express the unknown implacable which has endured life for so long by our reckoning and has now turned against it so implacably to wipe it out ...

The searching scepticism of the writer's philosophical analysis has established this Antagonist as invincible reality for him, but, all over the earth and from dates immemorial, introspective minds, minds of the quality of the brooding Shakespeare, have conceived a disgust of the stresses, vexations and petty indignities of life and taken refuge from its apprehension of a conclusive end to things, in mystical withdrawal. On the whole mankind has shown itself tolerant, sympathetic and respectful to such retreats. That is the peculiar human element in this matter; the recurrent refusal to be satisfied with the normal real world. The question 'Is this all?' has troubled countless unsatisfied minds throughout the ages, and, at the end of our tether, as it seems, here it is, still baffling but persistent ...

Hitherto, recurrence has seemed a primary law of life. Night has followed day and day night. But in this strange new phase of existence into which our universe is passing, it becomes evident that *events no longer recur.* They go on and on to an impenetrable mystery, into a voiceless limitless darkness, against which this obstinate urgency of our dissatisfied minds may struggle, but will struggle only until it is altogether overcome ...

Mind near exhaustion still makes its final futile movement towards that 'way out or round or through the impasse'.

That is the utmost now that mind can do. And this, its last expiring thrust, is to demonstrate that the door closes upon us for evermore.

There is no way out or round or through...

Our doomed formicary is helpless as the implacable Antagonist kicks or tramples our world to pieces.

This passage has been quoted at length because it gives a good idea of unconscious worship – admittedly a worship of fear and despair – which claims to derive from clear inquiry, but clearly does not do so. If the future is dark and the adversary unknowable, how can it be known that 'the door closes on us for evermore'? The supposed Antagonist cannot be implacably opposed to life, or it would never have been permitted to arise in the first place. This is a vision, not a rational conclusion. It is a vision of part of the cosmic process, and it is described vividly in the Eleventh Chapter of the Gita, where the Antagonist is met face to face. But it is only a part, and the same Chapter shows him as the Protagonist himself, the very life of the universe, upholding and sustaining it.

In one of the letters of the collection *Dear Bertrand Russell* (Allen & Unwin, London, 1969) Russell has this:

October 3, 1961

... As for the strange sympathy between Conrad and myself, I cannot pretend that I have ever quite understood it. I think I have always felt that there were two levels, one that of science and common sense, and another, terrifying, subterranean and periodic, which in some sense held more truth than the everyday view. You might describe this as a Satanic mysticism. I have never been convinced of its truth, but in moments of intense emotion it overwhelms me. It is capable of being defended on the most pure intellectual grounds – for example, by Eddington's contention that the laws of physics only *seem* to be true because of the things that we choose to notice. I suppose that the feeling I had for Conrad depended upon his combination of passion and pessimism – but that perhaps is a simplification.

These experiences are not unusual among those who regard themselves as sceptical. What is unusual is the frankness with which they are expressed by Wells and Russell. All this is worship; emotional and intellectual energy goes out to something which is hardly to be described, except that it is threatening; and in return the object of worship overwhelms the worshipper at times of deep emotion, as Russell says. The Gita calls it worship of the destructive power which is responsible for the breaking-down processes of the universe, but which is only a fragment of the great vision of the Lord.

Anything can become an object of worship, invested with a mysterious awe, which is never analysed but which demands concentration and service. The many legends of the dragon guarding a treasure – typified by Fafner in Wagner's *Ring* – are examples of worship. Why does the dragon guard the treasure? It is no use to him. Fafner is originally a giant, a master builder, but he becomes enslaved by a treasure, and in the end is simply a watchman, transformed into a dragon sleeping on it. The money is never spent or used; to the dragon its mere existence as a heap is enough. This is worship.

Karl Marx was rather reluctant to describe the consummation which he hoped for; he does say, however, that the organised state will wither away, leaving men to an Arcadian life. It is rather like the Garden of Eden, or certain passages of Taoist sages of China, and was clearly a vision which he worshipped.

But yoga tells us that these objects of worship have not been looked at steadily. If man analyses what he hopes for to the very end, he will find that he must become a god. All his formulations rest on unspoken assumptions – if he thinks money will satisfy him, he is always implicitly assuming that his health will hold up, that his friends will not be consumed with envy, that he will receive love, that no foreign invasion will come.

The yogi must penetrate through his assumptions and find something more real.

PRACTICE

The practice is to be done first of all in a meditation posture, preferably on a cushion or folded blanket on the floor, with one foot up on the opposite thigh and the other foot underneath, forming a triangle on which the body can be supported for a long time. Failing this, the practitioner may sit on a chair, but without supporting himself on the back of it.

The general posture of the back is something like that of a horseman looking into the distance. The spine is balanced, which means fairly straight, and the weight of shoulders and head should be felt to rest on the loins. Hands are locked together in some way, and eyes half shut or, if there is no tendency to sleep, fully closed. Westerners should cultivate where possible a seated position on the floor; it does not have associations of sleep for them and they can easily remain awake with eyes closed. The posture is much more difficult for Eastern people from those countries where they have sat on the floor from childhood, and been used to dropping off at odd moments. To Westerners, going to sleep often involves a ritual of going to bed; this fact makes meditation on the floor easier for them, so far as avoiding sleep is concerned.

To acquire a firm posture for meditation is a great advantage. For some people it is an absolute necessity. Passing thoughts and feelings are expressed by the face; longer-lasting moods by the movement or repose of the limbs; the fundamental attitude to life by the posture of the whole body, symmetrical and balanced or otherwise. Moreover, these expressions reinforce their causes, which is an important fact in training.

Someone who is worried or irritated by every triviality should sometimes face a mirror and slowly smooth the lines from the forehead till it is clear. Those who are professional worriers can use a rosary to repeat a mantra or a name of God silently, holding it somewhere at the centre line of the body, and keeping the other limbs still. One whose whole attitude to life is distorted should periodically bring the attention to the centre line of the body, the limbs into symmetry and the body straight; he should remain like that for a few minutes every so often. After some practice, the posture can be maintained in essentials during clerical work, and in many cases physical work also.

A traditional meditation posture frees from the reinforcing effects of bad physical habits or inner tensions. Seated in one such meditation posture, let the practitioner for at least half an hour try to search for what it is that he is worshipping – not necessarily in adoration, but in fear or anxiety if that is the case. It is his whole view of life and the universe that is in question. After at least half an hour of such analysis, which takes a good deal of courage, let him read one of the yogic or other books of revelation, to rouse an echo from the deepest layers of his being. If his analysis has been conducted with real determination, that echo is not too long in coming. When there is a stir, he will be able to face towards reality. The spiritual records call forth an answer because they are expressions of the truth of the human being. Deeper than the unconscious of Freud or the collective unconscious postulated by Jung, both of which are in the yogic classics included under 'darkness', is a God who is the projector of the universe. In the ordinary man he is as it were dreaming; concentration on the great spiritual sayings makes him stir – in fact the impulse to study them means that this aspect of God is already stirring.

Worship produces energisation and clarification of the mental processes, and a view of the world as purposeful. The worshipper becomes dimly aware of the part he is to play in that purpose, and can experience in himself the strength to play it. As his ship begins to move, he sees also that the water rises in seeming opposition; but to a worshipper it is no true opposition – the bow-wave is simply part of sailing. He finds that worship is not an infantile dependence, but a responsibility; to fulfil it requires everything he is. But he gradually becomes free from many of the disadvantages of the man who has no sense of a cosmic purpose; 'even a little of this yoga frees one from great fear.'

OM PRACTICE

The best method for worship, and ultimately for realisation of the Self, is to use the syllable Om. It belongs to no language – as Dr Shastri pointed out, it is not subject to the various grammatical modifications to which the ordinary Sanskrit words conform. In the Katha Upanishad, the teacher, who is the god of death, says:

> The word which all the Vedas declare, and what is said to be the end of all austerities, seeking which men lead a life of religion, that word I declare to you. It is Om.
>
> This syllable alone is Brahman; this syllable alone is the supreme; knowing this alone, whatever anyone wishes, that is his.
>
> This is the best support, this is the supreme foundation; knowing this foundation one enjoys bliss in the world of Brahman.

Shankara says elsewhere,

> Although the words Brahman, Atman and so on are names of Brahman, yet on the authority of the holy texts we know that Om is its nearest appellation. Therefore it is the best means for the realisation of Brahman.

It is used as a symbol, and as a name; yet it is more than these, for the Upanishads declare that Om *is* Brahman. The statement seems fantastic on the face of it, but it is not made for nothing.

Om is used in many traditions which have nothing to do with the Vedas; for instance some of the important chapters of the Koran have letters in front of them, whose meaning has been kept secret. Mohammad said, 'Every book has its secret, and this is the secret of the Koran.' The most important set of letters is

Alif, Lam, Mim, which in our alphabet correspond to A, L and M. Between A and M, an L is pronounced as U or double-U, which gives A U M – the same make-up of the word Om as is given in the Upanishads. (English people may remark that A + U come out to an O in Sanskrit, as they do in French – au revoir, au pair, and so on.)

In the Jewish tradition, the 'God of Amen' of Isaiah is a modern pronunciation of a word originally pronounced 'Omein'; when Christ says so often in the Authorised Version 'Verily, verily I say unto you' he was saying 'Omein, Omein, I say unto you'. In the Far Eastern Buddhist sects, especially the mantra sects, Om is one of the principal syllables for practice.

There are a number of other traditions which use Om, but the main point is practice, not piling up instances.

The three sutras of Patanjali on Om repetition are:

1.27 Om is his expressing-word

28 Repetition of it and meditation on its meaning

29 Thence realisation of a pure self within and disappearance of obstacles

In his commentary Shankara says:

Just as human gurus come to be before us when we devote ourselves to them, and give their grace to those who are wholly engaged in serving them, so this supreme Guru God gives his grace, as perfection in meditation. So the holy text says,

'He who has supreme devotion to God, and to the teacher as to God, From that Mahatma these glories shine forth.'

(Subala Upanishad) And the Gita:

'He who does works for Me, who looks on Me as the Supreme,

Who is devoted to Me, who is free from attachment,
Who is without hatred for any being,
He comes to Me, O Arjuna.' (XI.55)

Patanjali has said in sutra 23: From devotion to God also (samadhi comes about). Now how is one to be devoted to him, and by what means? To explain this, to show the method of devotion, the sutra now says 'Om is his expressing word'.

He goes on:

The Lord protects his devotees from sansara, he leads the sansarin to nirvana, he causes him to have unsurpassed joy, and by conferring samadhi, he gives him realisation. In every case the peak of devotion to the Lord is associated with truth, with the realisation 'the supreme truth is verily this'. Now the question arises, is the fact that Om expresses the Lord a conventional association, or is it something natural and permanent as the light is an expression of a lamp? One may say: Suppose that it is an ordinary name set up for convenience, perhaps from divine revelation or simply by men, in the form 'let us use Om as a name of God'. Previously to that, God would have been expressed by other names than Om, and the worshippers then would have been meditating upon him by some other sound or concentrated upon him by some other name. So they can do so still; what is specially important about Om? The answer is, that the power of Om to express the Lord is something permanent, like the light manifesting the lamp. So even at a first hearing of Om, the Lord is cognisable, like the sun by its light. It may be objected Worship that if this were so, the sutra 'Om is his expressing-word' would not have been necessary. It is just because the relation between Om and the Lord does not exist (naturally) that a conventional association is made by the sutra.

To this objection, the answer is: there is a permanent relation between the Lord and the Om expressing him ... The conventional association (pointed out in the sutra, simply) *lights up* the fixed relation (between the Lord and Om).

There follows a long technical discussion on whether names are arbitrarily chosen or not. The objector repeats his point that if the relation is permanent and not merely conventional, people should understand that Om expresses the Lord when they hear it for the first time. Shankara explains that the conventional association – the sentence 'his expressing-word is Om' – illumines or makes clear a permanent relation between the Lord and his expression Om, just as the conventional names 'father' and 'son' illumine an established father-son relation, which is a fact not dependent on names. On hearing 'that man is the father of the other one', the resemblance, etc. between them is noticed, which before perhaps had not been recognised.

So the conclusion is, whether one accepts the traditional view about names or not, either way there is here a fixed relation like that of father-and-son, and it is made manifest by the conventional association.

If there were no fixed relation between the Lord and this expressing-word, then it would not be correct that the Lord comes face to face with one by means of Om ... But if there is a fixed relation between the Lord and the expressing-word, then Om is an appropriate means as a practice for worshipping God, and this is what the doctrine wishes to teach.

When the yogi has thus understood the relation of expression (Om) and expressed (the Lord), what is the discipline which attracts the grace of the Supreme Lord to him? To explain this the sutra says: 'Repetition of it and meditation upon its meaning.' Repetition of Om which is the expression of the Lord is called japa, and it is repetition mentally or in a low voice. The repetition is made of Om considered as of three measures (A, U and M) or considered as of three-and-a-half measures (A, U, M and the soundless). Meditation upon its meaning: meditation is contemplation on the Lord, the meaning, held steady by the Om which is his expression. The meaning is thus implanted in the mind (buddhi). 'Is to be done' is to be supplied at the end of the sutra.

Yogis who are thus doing both (Om-repetition and meditation on the meaning) attain one-pointedness of mind. And that attainment of one-pointedness is a result of worship. There is a traditional verse:

Through Om-repetition let him practise yoga,
Through yoga, let him set his mind on Om;
By perfection in Om-repetition and in yoga
The Supreme Self shines forth clear.

Here are some comments on the phrases of this verse. *Through Om-repetition* through repetition of the syllable, having his mind bowed before the Lord,

let him practise yoga let him meditate on the Lord who is expressed by Om. And then, he whose mind has become unwavering as a result of his meditation on the Lord, who is the meaning of Om –

let him set his mind on Om let him repeat it mentally. Mental repetition is to be taken as the highest form, inasmuch as this verse associates Om-repetition with meditation (dhyana). The sense is that the mind must not run towards objects.

In this way, *by perfection in Om-repetition and in yoga* – a man who is undisturbed by other ideas opposed to them is one who is perfect in Om-repetition and in yoga – by that perfection in repetition of Om and meditation on the Supreme Lord, the *Supreme Self* (parama-atman) who stands above all *shines forth clear* to the yogi.

The next sutra is: 'Thence, realisation of a pure consciousness within, and disappearance of obstacles.' Holy Vyasa, at the beginning of his comments on this sutra, says: 'And what else happens to him?' This refers to the fact that one result has already been indicated, namely that Om-repetition produces one-pointedness of mind. Is that one-pointedness then the only result, or is there something else? The answer is given in the present sutra.

Thence from devotion to the Lord by Om practice; *pure consciousness within* means something which is aware of the mind (buddhi) itself, which is within; that consciousness is the Self;

realisation of it means recognition of one's own nature as it really is.

It may be objected: the self is already realised in everyone as the feeling 'I am an enjoyer' or 'I am a sufferer'. This is a universal experience; what is special about it? The answer is, that this is true, but this realisation is a confused idea in the mind. When a man says 'I am an enjoyer' and 'I am a sufferer', the 'enjoyer' and 'sufferer' refer to the same thing, for they are (mutually contradictory) thoughts about the bare notion 'here I am'. Thus it is clear that (being mutually contradictory) they are merely notions arising from Ignorance.

Like what, then is the Self realised to be? Like the Lord, who is Self, pure, radiant, alone, without evil, supreme, conscious.

This extended quotation from Shankara's commentary on the yoga sutras gives a good idea of the theory of Om practice. From its repetition, in a spirit of worship, as the expression of the Lord, there comes about perfect concentration in samadhi, removal of obstacles, a direct face-to-face vision of the Lord, and a realisation of the Self within. He says that Om is a natural expression of the Lord, and when it is repeated there is at once a relation with the Lord, but this has to be made clear by directing attention to it, in cases where confusions distract the mind in other directions.

Some modern teachers compare the process to using a radio set; Om-repetition corresponds to tuning the set to the desired wavelength, and the station is immediately received. But if in the vicinity there are numerous other electrical appliances in operation, the broadcast may hardly be recognisable because of interference. They have to be shut off, and attention directed to what is happening in the radio set.

It is a question of actually practising the repetition. Swami Rama Tirtha, a fellow-disciple of Dr Shastri and a great mahatma who was also a scientist, laid special emphasis on Om as the central practice of Vedanta. He gives many instructions about it in his lectures and writings. Here is one of them:

> When you sing this sacred mantram Om, you will have to throw your intellect and body into your true Self, and make these melt into the real Self. Realise it and sing in the language of feeling, sing it with your acts, sing it through every pore of your body. Let it course through your veins, let it pulsate in your bosom, let every hair on your body and every drop of your blood tingle with the truth that you are the Light of lights, the sun of suns, the ruler of the universe, the lord of lords, the true Self.

The yogis use strong phrases about Om. Dr Shastri says that all the forces of the universe are incorporated in it. These statements are not dogmas which a yogi must try to force himself to 'believe', though he secretly does not; still, they should not be quite forgotten. They are not said for nothing.

The yogi sits in a solitary place, in a firm upright yogic posture. He repeats Om with a rosary of 108 beads or knots, slowly; finally each Om takes about 15 seconds, including the in-breath. But there is no need to strive to lengthen it at first. If he concentrates on the physical sound produced in his throat and gives attention to it, after some weeks he begins to feel the vibration spread into the chest and further down, and also upward into the head. Let him put the attention on the downward- going vibrations. If he keeps upright and still, he will become aware of their spreading. At the beginning it is necessary for most people to be in a place where the Om can be repeated with a steady intonation, a strong vibrato (not a tremolo) and a well-prolonged MMMMMMMMMMMM at the end. But with some practice, as the body becomes more tranquil and the tensions lessen, there is awareness of the vibrations even of a gentle repetition. The body is felt to vibrate with it, like a cello. It is worthwhile finding an opportunity to lay a finger on a cello while it is being played. Though the vibration is invisible to the eye, there is a strong feel – this gives a hint for the Om practice.

'Chant Om with every fibre of your body.' It is not meant as a metaphor. One who chants Om in the meditation posture, upright and still, finds the tension relaxing; there is an appreciable effect by the end of eight minutes. Then he feels a sort of resonance which comes at first only occasionally, something like the resonance which a man experiences who sings in a small space like a bathroom. The repeater of Om feels it more clearly as his hardness softens and his attention sharpens.

If we hold down the middle C on a piano, without sounding it, and then strike a low C double-forte and staccato, we find that the middle C is softly sounding, though it has not been struck. It would be the same if a C below the ear's range were sounded; the middle C within our aural range would still sound, though for no apparent reason. Om repetition tunes our physical instrument, so to speak, and after some weeks or months the repeater becomes aware that along with the Om which he himself is saying, another Om is sounding in him. The instrument has been tuned by deliberate sounding, but when it has been tuned, it will sound even though not sounded. In Zen it is referred to in the koan, 'Of the one hand, what sound would there be?'

Repetition of Om, using the perception of the sound, in the end produces a sort of double consciousness. There is the ordinary perception of body, and the awareness 'here I am sitting at this time and this place'. But along with that, there is a consciousness of the sound, long, drawn-out, vibrating in certain parts of the body and finally throughout the whole body, and a feeling that besides the Om being uttered, there is another Om, felt as an added resonance. This other Om seems to be 'heard', but not as a vibration through the air; it seems to be an addition to the uttered Om, heard through the flesh and bones of the body. There are various descriptions of the experience, but there is no point in collecting them. It is a question of experiment, and the experience when it does come is not what had been imagined from the descriptions. Not that the latter were wrong, but they are always mixed up with the pre-conceptions of the reader, and so his imagined anticipations are faulty.

Suppose a yogi takes one of the verses of the Chapter of the Self, to use with repetition of Om.

The world is not different from him, who is ever standing as the supreme, who is to be known, who himself divides into many. From him the bodies all come forth, he is the root, eternal, he is constant.

He meditates on the meaning of this text, and then sums up that meaning in Om. Om is the expression of that Lord, as the voice or the strength are the expression of the man. He repeats Om with this conviction, which is sometimes steady, and sometimes has to be again and again renewed. After some weeks of repetition for, say, an hour a day, some of the super-impositions (adhyasa in Shankara's term) of place and time and cause-and-effect begin to lessen. They become thinner, so to say. The sound as expression of God fills more and more of the forefront of waking consciousness; the feeling 'I am saying Om' becomes intermittent, and in its place is an experience of Om as divine universal energy and so-to-say parenthood, with himself in it. He feels that his body is beginning to dissolve in Om, that he is Om. The meditation is then going into samadhi.

A final point about the practice is that, as Shankara says, mental repetition is the best. Most people cannot achieve it at once: their minds wander. At first repetition needs to be fairly clear, otherwise the characteristic Om 'feeling' is not noticed because of tension in muscles and nerves. But this is only at the beginning. Fundamentally the practice is not a question of drowning inner tension by a thunder of sound, as in some mostly primitive sects which have almost no discipline of refining the psychological instruments. Such a practice can be harmful to the instrument, because it is against its nature; it corresponds to working in wood across the grain instead of studying its constitution and following the natural lines. In yoga, practice is along the true lines of development, which have been studied minutely. Forcing a thing instead of studying and following its nature is painful and often fruitless, both in yoga and in the world.

For example, if a radio set is not properly tuned, there is noise along with the desired programme. The programme can be received more loudly by increasing the volume, but it is not heard more clearly because the noise increases also. And so very loud and excited repetition of mantras may be an attempt to drown internal or external interference by volume of noise. Some spiritual perceptions may be experienced, but the deep-seated vasana complexes – of power or sex or vanity – are also heightened, and they distort the experience. They are parasitic elements, as some Christian mystics call them.

There has to be some force in the Om practice at first, or else it can tail off into daydreaming. But the aim is to still and clarify inner awareness, and then the Om is to be perceived more and more as an 'inner' sound. When sleepy, or assailed by distractions, or even out of exuberance of spiritual joy, Om may be pronounced loudly or sung, as Rama Tirtha used to shout it echoing in the Himalayan valleys; but that is not the essence of the practice. Abu Bakr used to repeat the name of God quietly, Omar repeated it loudly. When the Prophet, whose disciples they were, was asked about it, he said, 'Omar is in the stage of purification, while Abu Bakr is in the stage of contemplation.'

If worship through the Om practice or any other practice is successful, the yogi feels something of the expression of the Lord in himself. But till what Shankara calls the stage of 'right vision' is reached, this does not yet affect the fundamental conviction of being a separate individual. When he comes out of meditation, he has a memory which is a great support in life, but it is not yet a clear experience of identity. He is still a karma yogi, moving towards Knowledge, but not yet wanting to jump into it.

10. Free Action

The second part of karma-yoga is 'performing one's duty without attachment to the fruits of the actions'. The word which is translated 'fruit' can be rendered 'result', but the first is better because it implies a distance from the action, and this is the sense of the Sanskrit. If a fruit tree is planted, the result of the action is that the tree stands there in the ground; the fruit comes much later.

To perform an action without attachment to the fruit does not mean without caring whether it is done well or badly. When cleaning a brass pot, or making a speech, a yogi is not to do it carelessly; with the brass he must rub evenly and vigorously, and with the speech he must prepare it with a definite structure, and speak firmly. He must not do these things badly and then say, 'I did not care about the fruit.' To leave the pot dull, to deliver a confused speech hesitatingly, is not doing the action at all. A pot half dirty has not been cleaned; a confused and uncertain farrago is not a speech at all. What is technically called the 'fruit' of these actions would be praise from a neighbour at the shining brass, or even a sense of self-congratulation at how well it had been done, or the applause of the audience for the speech. The test of detachment would be that when the action fails – someone upsets coffee over the pot, or the audience is hostile because they do not like what has been said – then he is not disturbed; similarly if there is success, he is not elated.

Detached action is done as energetically as action which is powered by strong desire; Shankara cites the Gita on this:

As the ignorant act who are caught up in their own interests, so should the wise man perform action, but untouched, and for the good of the world ... He should encourage the ignorant to perform right actions, and himself perform them with energy and skill.

As a matter of fact, the yogic agent who is free from involvement in a distant 'fruit' can do better than one who is caught up. The *worst* agent is the lazy man who does not want to do anything at all; he prefers where possible to leave things as they are, for fear of what might happen. The *next* best agent is the man of passion-struggle, who does actions partly to get definite advantages which he desires, and partly to feel in himself the power of overcoming obstacles. He often fails, however, because his excitement makes him try to force things, and also requires him to take a leading role all the time. The *highest* agent is the one who is not passionately caught up with some future fruit but performs the action in the joy of the cosmic purpose, unmoved whether it succeeds or fails in the short run.

The notion of acting vigorously and yet without desire for a fruit is peculiarly difficult to understand for some cultures, but in those which have a tradition of sport, it is easily understood. The essence of sport is to try very hard; there is no savour where one side does not make a fight of it, on the ground that 'it is only a game'. And yet there is no exulting in victory nor depression in defeat; in fact the struggle is to be a means of making friends, not enemies. A good sportsman appreciates a fine shot by his opponent as much as one of his own.

The chess master Edward Lasker relates that when he first came to London, he played a few games at the City of London chess club; one of them he won in brilliant fashion with a startling queen sacrifice. He says in one of his books:

I am sure none of the onlookers realised what a deep impression my opponent made on me when, on being checkmated, he smiled and shook hands with me. He said: 'This was very nice.' Only after Dr Schumer had translated these words to me, and had slowly repeated my adversary's name, did I realise that I had been playing the champion of London, Sir George A. Thomas. For him to take this defeat so graciously, was a fine example of sportsmanship. It was an attitude which I had hardly ever experienced during the years I had lived in Berlin. Had I won this game against one of the leading amateurs there, probably his only comment would have been: 'You are just lucky! Had I played 10 ... B x Kt instead of Q - K2, you would have been lost.'

The so-called sportsmanship was derived from chivalry, which took these attitudes into the whole of life. Or at least, that was the ideal, and we know that though many of the knights were brutal illiterates, there were some, and not only Christians, who made serious attempts to live it. Saladin sent a doctor to cure his great opponent Richard the Lionheart; some even say he came to visit him himself.

Robert, son of William the Conqueror, lost his chance of the throne of England by chivalrously refusing to lay siege to a key city when he learned that the queen was in the city and about to bear a child.

Green, in his *Medieval Civilization in Western Europe*, cites an extraordinary instance of allegiance to the chivalric code, overriding all other consideration. During Henry V's wars with France, Henry's brother, Humphrey, Duke of Gloucester, bribed a French captain to surrender the town of Cherbourg to the English. The captain was given a safe conduct to travel to his home, but was apprehended by the English at Rouen, tried by the orders of Henry V for accepting money (though from the English) which led him to betray his liege lord the King of France, was found guilty and executed, in spite of the fact that the treason he had committed was at the behest of the English and to the English advantage. Moreover, the trial and sentence would prevent the English from benefiting from treachery in the future.

The Romans in early days had their own chivalric code, which treated even crucial battles as somehow under rules, like a sport. Even up to the second century B.C. there were those who would not countenance such 'tricks' and 'cleverness' as ambushes or night attacks.

Nearly all sportsmen find that they play worse if there is some valuable prize for which they are competing, or even a large audience to whom a failure would look ridiculous. Attachment to the 'fruit' creates tension, which impairs the technique. A Confucian saying is: 'When the archers shoot for a clay prize, they shoot well; if for silver, badly; if it is gold they are as if blind.' There are a few, amateurs or professionals, who can practice detachment in their sport. A golf champion was asked how he approached a critical shot when everything depends on it. He replied, 'I have found that the only way is to play the shot and not try to play the situation; I have to forget the situation in a sort of cocoon of concentration, and then I can play the shot well. If I feel the situation, I often make a mess of the shot.'

There are many such accounts in different fields, but often this detachment is only within the chosen speciality, and not available for life in general.

As to 'duty' it does not mean something imposed and accepted reluctantly, as opposed to what one really wants to do. The word translated duty really means 'what is to be done', and the yogas listed as virtues in the Chapter of the Self are expressions of the true Self of man, not unnatural rules precariously holding down a volcano of passions, as in the vision of Russell which he felt was shared also by Conrad. They are 'what is to be done' in the sense that full and regular breathing is what is to be done by the asthmatic; when a suggestion is given to remedy his emotional spasm, it is given in such terms as 'breathe slowly, breathe in relaxation, breathe fully'. These instructions, apparently in conflict with what he feels he can do, are the proper, natural way of breathing; in a sense they are followed as something imposed from outside, but really they are restoring the natural function on the deepest level.

The aspects of duty are set out in the law-books for the ordinary man, but the special yogas, for the one who seeks liberation, are given at the end of the Chapter of the Self, and they correspond closely to various lists in the Gita. Shankara's glosses on particular words like 'control' are almost word for word the same in the two commentaries. This is another indication of their close connection.

In the Gita, men are divided into four classes, but these divisions are not based on birth but on the character of the individual's attitude and conduct.

The natural actions of the Brahmin are proper to the qualities with which he is born: serenity, control, tapas (austerity), purity, forgiveness, straightforwardness, knowledge, spiritual realisation, and faith. All this is the natural duty of a Brahmin.

Bravery, majesty, firmness, being equal to any occasion, not frightened at opposition, generosity, authority – all this is the natural duty of a warrior.

Skill in agriculture, cattle-rearing and trade – this is the natural duty of the merchant.

Service is the natural duty of a shudra.

In the Gita, and in the Mahabharata epic generally, of which it is a part, there are many passages to show that membership of these classes is not simply from birth in a particular family. 'Truthfulness, giving, freedom from hatred and wickedness, humility, kindness, tapas – where these are seen, that man is a Brahmin. If these are found in a shudra, and not found in a Brahmin, then the shudra is no shudra and the so-called Brahmin is not a Brahmin.' And again, 'A Brahmin who is not a spiritual man, and an elephant made of wood – there is nothing there but the name.'

Obviously in a merchant family, mercantile ability in the children will very easily find scope, and similarly with the other classes. Imitation is a powerful force in education, and the father was there as a teacher. But there is nothing inevitable about it. There may be inherited abilities which the parents have not developed in themselves, and in any case the yogic view is that the mind, being in touch with the cosmic mind, is almost infinite, is not absolutely determined in its scope. However, by a process similar to that by which some geneticists come to believe that an 'instinctive' preference in First World War generals for horses over tanks could have been genetically, not socially determined, the view grew up in Hindu society that a person's role in life was determined by inheritance – 'caste' as the Europeans called it. Dr Shastri and his teacher were strongly opposed to this idea. The teacher, himself a Brahmin of a most distinguished lineage, insisted that his high-caste pupils should sometimes serve tea to shudra pupils, thus reversing the roles for the purpose of spiritual training. He used to point out to his pupils that the incarnation Rama, emperor of India, had among his closest friends the 'monkey' Hanuman, a member of one of the aboriginal tribes of India. These views nearly cost him his life.

The 'Brahmin' is one who knows, or wishes to know, Brahman, and his duty is to be a man of Brahman, to keep alight the flame of knowledge, spiritual realisation and faith, and to demonstrate it in his own life as truthfulness, kindness, and absolute independence. In this way he is a teacher of men. Some Brahmins demonstrated fearlessness by becoming wandering renunciates, without any property and living by begging, never staying more than three nights in one place.

The 'warrior' is a man of passion-struggle mixed with spiritual awareness, and he protects the order of society, by protecting the weak against the wolves and tigers in human form who would make a jungle out of it. The merchant is skilful in producing wealth for the community and himself; he supports the Brahmin, and pays taxes to the warrior, in return for spiritual light and material protection respectively. The Brahmin's role is of supreme importance in civilising the aggressive and acquisitive drives of the warrior and merchant, which otherwise lead to a delight in conquest or in piling up wealth, as absolute values and not as service.

The fourth class is the role of service. This is for someone who does not feel equal to standing alone in life; he wants help and protection, and he joins a group which contains those whom he feels he can look up to; he gives his loyalty and service to this group.

The shudra is not an exploited serf or slave, but a voluntary servant. As a matter of fact every spiritual student carries out this role at some time in his life, and it is to be noted that many of the poet-saints of India, like the great geniuses Tulsidas and

Surdas, had names ending in '-das', which means a servant. St Paul has a famous sentence, 'whose service is perfect freedom'. The riddle in this phrase often disappears through a mental trap door into oblivion, but no one can understand yogic training who has not at least partially solved it.

11. Independence of the Opposites

The third element in karma-yoga is independence of the pairs of opposites, heat and cold, pleasure and pain, and so on. The Gita verse (2.14) says that sense-contacts cause heat and cold, pleasure and pain; they come and go, being impermanent. They are to be endured bravely. And the next verse says, 'The wise man whom these do not afflict, to whom pleasure and pain are the same, he can attain immortality.'

The first pair, heat and cold, typify sense experience; the second pair are to exemplify inner reactions. Shankara's view is that in the first pair, the senses report heat or cold, and the mind (buddhi) modifies itself accordingly; Self is aware of the mental modification, and in the ignorant man there is a false identification with the modification – 'I am hot, I am cold'.

In the second case, there is a mental modification in the form of, say, pain, arising as a reaction to some stimulus inner or outer; a second mental modification witnesses this one, and the Self, witnessing that, is identified through Ignorance with it – 'I am suffering'.

The method of practising brave endurance of the first kind of opposite is called tapas (literally 'heat'); the method of practising brave endurance of the second kind of opposite is called vairagya (literally 'dispassion').

As to the first pair of opposites, heat and cold, Madhusudana's commentary on the Gita contains a semi-humorous protest, which is yet an accurate analysis of the real feelings: 'How can I be asked to do this? Don't we put on thick clothes when we are cold, and take them off again in the heat? Don't we protect ourselves against hunger and against thorns and so on? We all do these things. If we don't, we shall die. What is all this about independence of the pairs of opposites?'

The answer is: Yes, everyone does these things, and the yogi too eats and sleeps and wears clothes. But when the man of Ignorance cooks food and puts on clothes, he believes that these things protect him, and that nothing else will; therefore he piles them up. But in spite of all his precautions, he gets ill and catches cold, and in the end dies. The yogi when he lives relies on the Lord, the inner ruler of everything, and he uses only the minimum of things to support his life. As a result, he is much more vigorous, and he is not a prey to anxiety; if the things cease to be available, he does not feel he has lost his only support. He still relies on the Lord, and if it is time to die, he is conscious of immortality.

There is a saying of much wisdom: 'One bowl of rice and a vegetable is necessary each day; two is better; three is luxury; four makes him ill; five kills him.' Our Western civilisation is already at the stage of four, and it is time to give up piling up unnecessary things in our lives as a kind of superstitious charm. It is not just a question of food.

How is he to practise? The first thing is to reduce life needs to sensible levels, and to practise independence even of these. To practise independence means occasionally to fast, or remain awake one night in meditation and devotion; above all it means to be able to accept it without grumbling when the meal expected is not forthcoming, or a night's sleep has to be foregone. Our pre-conceptions about the needs of life need to be examined. These days we are free from the obsession with food, because it is recognised that over-eating rich foods leads to illness; the habit of rich Roman epicures of eating a banquet, vomiting it up again in a separate room, and then returning to eat another banquet seems to us disgusting. But we have our own obsessions, for instance a belief that culture can only be advanced by human beings completely sexually satisfied all the time. This arises from a sort of 'Freudian' mis-reading of what Freud actually wrote. In his *Beyond the Pleasure Principle*, for example, he says, 'The restless striving towards further perfection which may be observed in a minority of human beings is easily explicable as the result of that repression of instinct upon which what is most valuable in human culture is built.' The Yoga-sutra declares, 'From establishment in sexual restraint, attainment of energy', and Freud says almost the same thing – 'from the tension ... resulting from repression of instinct ... is born the driving momentum which allows of no abiding in any situation presented to it, but in the poet's words "urges ever forward, ever unsubdued" (Goethe's *Faust*, Act 1)'.

The second practice is to acquire a meditation posture, and gradually become relaxed and easy in it. By habituating the body and senses to control, mind can become more and more free from their domination. 'By relaxation of effort, and entering samadhi on infinity, the posture is perfected, and then the opposites no longer affect him' – these are two sutras of Patanjali, and Shankara comments, 'When the posture has become firm, this follows as a result, that he is not overcome by pairs of opposites like heat and cold.'

The yogi sitting in the meditation posture feels and meditates that all is space. This is now easier for anyone who has a smattering of science, which informs us that the amount of anything that can be called matter in an atom corresponds to three bees in the dome of St Paul's. Such statements do nothing to get rid of the experience of being a body, but they do help meet the objection, 'after all science vouches for the existence of solid matter, so how can one meditate on the body and the universe as space?' The yogi has to meditate on space till the meditation begins to go into samadhi, and he feels 'I am space'. When this happens he is hardly aware of the body or what happens to it – in some meditation experiences the body is still perceived, but as transparent.

Sometimes a yogi should practice endurance of cold and heat – not so much deliberately seeking them out, but meeting them with calm and without trying to run away when they arise in ordinary life. Every yogi, says Shankara, must perform some physical tapas, which reduces the doshas or impurities in him, and helps to bring samadhi. The true and direct adversary of Ignorance, he says, is direct vision (samyag-darshana) but tapas helps to remove the obstacles to right vision. 'It is fasting and so on, and endurance of heat and cold and other opposites.' The objector says, 'What has this physical tapas got to do with meditation, which is a mental thing?' The reply is:

Of a man without tapas, the yoga is not perfected. The yoga is not perfected of one whose mind is taken up with attending to his body and possessions, whose body senses and mind are lazy, who is always running away, who is always conscious of himself as a body, who thinks of himself as very delicate. This is the use of tapas ... Without tapas there is no destruction of the mass of latent impressions which have accumulated from time without beginning, and of a mind which still has this impurity, where is the samadhi?

The yogi must therefore give earnest attention to performing some tapas, but not (fanatical self-torture which would) disturb the calm of the mind. Since the purpose of the tapas is calm of the mind, if it disturbs the mind, its very purpose would be contradicted.

The yogi is not to torture himself physically, but he does perform exercises in tapas which invigorate him and produce mental calm. As an example: a lazy man who suddenly set himself to run ten miles would collapse. His tapas should be to run a little till he is tired, every day; the next week a little more, and finally after two or three years he can perform the tapas of running ten miles. To be able to keep up such a programme is a great tapas, not only of the body but the mind. Some days it will be raining, or he will feel he has a headache, and to persist with his run will give him a good degree of independence of the opposites.

At the end he may find that it is not a tapas any more, but a source of new life. The traditional forms of tapas all conduce in the end to vigour; they are never destructive of the instrument, but they establish mastery over it.

Different is independence from the inner reactions like pleasure and pain; the means to it is called vairagya. The word means literally absence of raga, which has the sense of colour, especially red as Shankara remarks, and hence passion, vehemence, hankering, anger and so on. A desire to win in an argument is not necessarily raga, but if it becomes vehement so that there is exultation when winning, and fury when losing, then it is. The root in Sanskrit has the sense of dyeing – cloth of a neutral colour is dyed a violent red; in the same way actions and feelings can become 'charged' with passion. Raga is sometimes contrasted with dvesha or aversion; but as a rule raga stands for both hankering and aversion, both of them being passionate and based on an intense interest in the object.

Vairagya is detachment from the objects of the world, and further from the gunas or qualities which are the basis of particular objects. We are related to objects and to gunas by false desire and false aversion, both based on a wrong conception of the Self and of the object or guna. All desires, except the desire for God, are false.

The main means to vairagya are:

philosophical analysis,
learning through experience of disappointment,
creating a master sentiment which pulls the currents of life into a harmonious flow,
expanding selfish desires into universal art,
science and benevolence,
samadhi meditation,
vision of Self,
and grace of God.

We will look at them in turn.

Philosophical analysis tells us that our desires do not necessarily correspond to our true needs. A man suffering from one form of diabetes has an intense thirst, but a drink relieves it for only a moment. The need is for insulin, which his body is no longer manufacturing in sufficient quantities. He does not consciously desire insulin, in fact he may never have heard of it; the need is expressed, falsely, as a desire to drink and drink.

The practice consists in removing the idea that any desire represents an absolute value. A man in the cold naturally desires to be warmer, but if he is on an important errand to help someone in need, he simply brushes the desire aside. A mountaineer takes pleasure in challenging the onrush of desires for comfort and safety and warmth. Even life itself does not have absolute value. Some yogas stress the point that no man can be really free until he can willingly give up his life for a noble cause. Life only has meaning as a means to realisation of God; merely to live, even centuries as a turtle was supposed to do, has no meaning.

Among the classical defects in the objects which have to be repeatedly considered are, their passing nature, the labour which is involved in getting and keeping them, and the hatred by people who are in an inferior position. This sort of analysis drives towards seeing that the apparent objects are based on a 'false notion' (mithya-jnana), a phrase which Shankara often uses. The Chapter of the Self commentary explains that unless it is realised that the doshas rest on a false notion, and unless the yoga practice is based upon right vision, it cannot be guaranteed that the yogas will overcome the doshas.

Pleasure attained from an object soon loses its keenness; it used to be said humorously by sailors that when a man has been rescued from a raft, it is only a week before he is complaining about the coffee served on the ship which has rescued him. As to getting and guarding, it is significant how in many fairy stories a man obtains a treasure but cannot enjoy it; he becomes merely a mindless guardian of it. The treasure has obtained the man; he dies defending it. In the Islamic tradition it is said: They asked the Prophet what he had to say about the things of the world. He replied: 'What can I say about them? Things acquired with much effort, guarded with constant anxiety, and left finally with regret.'

This kind of analysis does not mean that a yogi must not strive for success in the tasks which engage him. He does strive, and with great energy. Because he is balanced in mind and heart, he is often more successful than others, a fact which may or may not be resented. But in any case he does not believe that success will give him lasting pleasure. He does the actions simply because they ought to be done, he makes a special point of sharing the fruits of any success with others, and he is not upset when they go. Nor is he upset if the whole undertaking ends in failure.

The commentator Vyasa gives sex, self-preservation, and power as examples of objects causing binding attachment, and Shankara remarks that though there is an infinity of objects causing desire, yet the principal impulse of raga is above all grasping after these three. In these cases raga is at its most powerful, and it is to be opposed with the greatest determination.

The nature of the satisfaction and fulfilment momentarily felt on attaining a much-longed-for object has been minutely analysed by Indian philosophers. The conclusion is that concentration on one object leads to temporary suppression of all other desires, and a narrowing-down till the object represents the whole world. When it is attained, for a moment it is felt that the whole world has been attained – the man momentarily feels himself a god. The mind is calm in the feeling 'all that was to be attained has been attained'. But very soon the suppressed desires and anxieties begin to sprout up, as the concentration becomes dispersed. Then it is found that the whole world has not been attained; the absolute value which concentration had superimposed on the chosen object is found to be only relative value after all. There is often a great sense of disillusionment.

(From the yogic point of view, dispelling of illusion is a great advantage; it can release the energy which has been locked up in preserving the illusion by concentration. But the man of the world hates disillusionment; illusion is his life, and his death also.)

In Shankara's commentary on Patanjali, the point is repeatedly made that these same considerations apply even to the heavens enjoyed by the gods and by those who worship them.

The gods enjoying great powers are still subject periodically to envy and to fear. They are not liberated, and their state of glory is only temporary. When their favourable karma is exhausted, they are thrown down to the state of mortals again, and their places are taken by others who have earned a similar temporary elevation.

Some people can learn vairagya through *experience of disappointment*. This is a path of agony, and no one should deliberately take it. And there are those who never learn even from bitter disappointment, but persuade themselves that all will be different next time. People of sincere feeling can come to yoga through distress, and what the world calls disaster is an opening, if it can be taken. At such times the conviction that nothing in the world is worthwhile produces a release of power. It generally dissipates itself in futile regrets and remorse, or sometimes in anger, but if the energy can be re-directed into yogic practice, it leads to progress in a short time. It should be expected, however, that when after a little yogic practice the keen edge of grief disappears, there is a danger of forgetting, and again taking up the pursuit of false aims. This can happen again and again.

A partial vairagya can be attained by cultivating a *master sentiment* (a phrase of William James which Dr Shastri often used). A keen musician, for instance, who must practise several hours a day, is immune from the habit of watching television for long periods. He feels restless if he has to do so, and the programmes seem to him a waste of time. If the master sentiment is study of yoga philosophy, or the practice of singing devotional songs, it can be an important step on the path, and frees the yogi from many inner and outer adhesions. But the detachment so produced is still only partial – there may be pride of learning, or self-complacency in devotion. In such cases the vairagya is what

Shankara calls the second stage, where some binding desires have been transcended but not others.

However, except in cases where a yogi from a temporary timidity deliberately holds back and takes refuge in his existing state, the concentration does bring a new insight, which will modify the master sentiment. Ultimately the quest for truth takes possession. When this happens, irrelevant attitudes and irrational compulsions begin to lose their force. To organise the master sentiment, Dr Shastri recommended that at the beginning at least one hour a day must be given to yogic practice and study, and some yogic unselfish benevolence must be performed to release the cramp of individuality. After some time, at least three hours a day must be given to yoga. Those who do this are able to live without the internal whirlpools which overwhelm action and judgment; there may be eddies, but in general their actions are well balanced and effective.

Expansion of selfish desires into universal sympathy, and creativity in art and science and benevolence, is an allied process. Desire cannot be suppressed by a mere order of the will; it may seem to disappear but it comes up in another form, often obvious to a third party but hidden from oneself. To transform desire there must be active pursuit of a great ideal, without a sense of possessiveness. There are those who make sacrifices for a cause, but require that their sacrifices be known and appreciated. This is not transformation of selfish desire but a re-direction of it, and often no improvement. The true virtue is what the Chinese yogis call 'hidden virtue', which no one knows about; in the end the man himself is to become unaware of his own virtue, and this is the true virtue which has the power to transform the environment.

In the Middle Ages in Japan, there was a movement for reciting the name of the Buddha of Light in groups. One of the leaders of this movement was Honen, who chanted the name of Buddha in all the towns and villages. In one small town, when the party came and chanted in the streets, among the bystanders was a local thief and one of his henchmen. The junior was impressed and said so to his chief. 'I don't like it,' replied the other, 'after all it's just a circus. They say their purpose is to adore the Buddha, but it isn't is it? Their purpose is to let us see them adoring the Buddha, and that isn't an adoration at all. After all, if I fell in love with a woman I might tell her how much I cared for her, but it would be whispered into her ear. If I shouted her name in public and said all those things in the street, it wouldn't be affection at all, would it?'

As it happened, Honen put up at the same cheap inn where the thief happened to be staying. The latter got up in the middle of the night and crept round the verandah to peep into Honen's room. He saw him sitting in front of a tiny light, and repeating the name of the Buddha of Light in a whisper. The thief watched for some time but Honen continued doing the same thing. Then the thief sneezed, and Honen immediately blew out the light and lay down.

The thief crept back to his own room. Next day he spoke to Honen and told him all that had happened. Honen said, 'You are right that our recitation in public is not the real adoration of Buddha. We do it so that people may be attracted to do it themselves; that is a holy purpose, but it is not real adoration. Real adoration is done when no one knows about it. When you sneezed, I knew someone was watching me, and from that moment my adoration would have had no spiritual value. So I stopped, and waited till I should be alone again.'

The thief became one of Honen's followers.

Samadhi practice is to touch directly the latent desires which dwell in the causal layer, the seed-bed so to say of thoughts and feelings which are available to our inspection. We do not know what desires may be dormant there. A commentator gives the example of Maitra who is in love with one woman; other women however beautiful seem uninteresting to him. This does not mean his desire for them is extinct; it is merely dormant, temporarily over-ruled, so that he does not feel it. In the same way a rich man may fancy himself honest – in fact he may *be* honest, having no need to be otherwise. But when circumstances change, he may find out whether his honesty was from conviction, or whether it was simply a habit like any other habit, liable to be modified under stress.

As will be explained, samadhi is the third step in meditation. The first is called dharana, holding the attention on to one place. The second is dhyana, when the attention rests there continuously, and does not have to be recalled with more or less frequency, as it does in dharana. But the meditator is still aware, 'I am meditating on this'. In samadhi, the 'I am meditating' vanishes, and the object, 'this', becomes radiant and blazes up in its own light; it is the whole universe.

The practice will be explained in Chapter 20, under the fourth item of karma-yoga.

Vairagya comes from *vision of the Self.* Even a glimpse of the Self frees from many long-standing obsessions. They are not exactly conquered triumphantly; they simply lose their importance because they become illusory. It is by vision of the Self that attachment even for the gunas is conquered. The ordinary man feels raga as attachment for specific objects, and the philosophical analysis and other practices are in the beginning directed mostly against this attachment for particular objects. But there is a much more subtle attachment, which is for the gunas themselves; it is different from attachment for objects. Take the guna rajas – passion-struggle. Normally this is felt as the fight for success in a particular thing; that thing is the object of attachment and joy is hoped for when it is attained. But a man whose attachment is for rajas itself does not mind much what thing it is that he fights for. His joy is in the struggle, and when he is successful he is rather indifferent to the object. It was merely a field for his rajas. Such men are mountaineers in everything. It is not that there is anything at the top of the mountain; they simply wish to 'conquer' it, as they put it. In the world they are often magnanimous to those whom they have defeated; it is victory itself that they want, not any particular success. Other people, travelling in the wake of such conquerors, may reap benefits, but the heroes themselves frequently waste their lives.

In the same way a man can be attached to the lethargy of tamas, which gives him a cheerful indifference to everything; or to the serenity and clarity of the individual self in sattva, which he does not wish to break up in favour of expansion into the unknown depths of the real Self.

The last way, which however cannot be employed in those yogas like the Jaina which rely on self-power alone, is *grace of God*. Shankara lays stress on this, especially in his Gita commentary. The grace is attracted by the efforts of the disciple, if those efforts are directed towards transcending his individuality. At the beginning a yogi tends to set up some ideal of his own: that he may be virtuous, may be loyal, may be eloquent in spreading the truth, may be compassionate, and so on. This picture has been selected from the basis of his individuality as he feels it to be – it is often a compensation for a feeling of inadequacy. As he makes progress, he begins to abandon these ambitions of spiritual childhood. He prays not that his inner being may find expression in one of these things selected by itself, but that it may be transformed into what the divine seeks to express through him. That may be something which he cannot conceive at present. Or if he could conceive it, it may seem to him something inferior.

When a savage prays to his god, he will ask for strength to conquer his enemies and protect his family and tribe, for skill in agriculture or hunting so that his people may be fed, and so on. The notion of forgiveness of enemies, or hospitality to strangers from another tribe, will not occur to him if it is not in his tradition. And if they are suggested to his mind, he will tend to despise them as based on weakness. Yet this is the true ideal in every man, as Christ and Buddha taught.

By repetition of the name of God and meditation on its meaning, and by prayer, the cramp of desire can be loosened. Such prayers are often apparently not answered for a time, because the disciple unconsciously may not in fact be too willing that the change should take place. But if he continues to struggle, there comes a bursting out, which he knows by the falling away of bonds which have held him prisoner for many years. He may, however, hardly be aware of the operation of divine grace till it is over.

A young monk by chance encountered the daughter of a wealthy merchant when her father brought her to visit his temple. They were overwhelmed with love for each other, as they believed it to be. The thought came to him to give up his profession, and try to enter the business and marry her. He knew her father would take her next morning to their own part of the country.

In the night he got up and prayed in the sanctuary to be freed from the temptation, but it became stronger and stronger. He repeated the holy name but it had no effect on his mind. Finally in the middle of his tears he fell asleep.

When he saw the morning spring sun shining in through the door he knew what he had to do. Without any preparations he went and quietly joined the merchant's party, lending a hand with the baggage. He became an apprentice in the business, and showed extraordinary ability. The father took to him, and made him his chief assistant; soon he asked permission to marry the daughter and the father agreed. They wed and had a child; the father died and he managed the business with outstanding success. Then an illness carried off both his wife and child, and he was prostrated with sorrow. He began to interest himself in charitable activities, first as a means of distracting himself from his grief, and later for their own sake. Then a series of accidents ruined the business and he was penniless. He became a pilgrim, and wandered round the country, trying to teach organisation and mutual help to the poor. He also tried to tell them that satisfaction of worldly desires alone would not lead to lasting happiness, but he had not the spiritual training and force which could carry conviction.

One evening he found himself near his former temple, and stole quietly in. Now an old and broken man, he prostrated himself and prayed for forgiveness. He asked only that the remainder of his life might be devoted to the good of all in any way the Lord might direct.

Again he fell asleep. Again he saw the morning sun shining in through the doorway. He found himself a young man once more, and realised it had all been a dream. But the desire had fallen away from him, and with the enormous access of energy released, he threw himself into his yogic practices and holy study. He became a spiritual light who influenced life in all that part of the country. Through grace, he experienced in a single night what would otherwise have occupied a whole life. In the same way, through grace, one tiny incident can give volumes of experience; what to another person would be almost nothing can be the turning point of a life. Of all the ways, the path of devotion to the Lord is the easiest, so says the Gita. To students of real sincerity, the stones and the fires and the animals reveal transcendental truth, as it is related in the Chandogya Upanishad. The Lord can speak through anything. In one way or another he lights the flame of Self-realisation in a devotee, and then the desires of the world thin out. Shankara concludes his exposition of the subject with the words, 'The highest vairagya is no other than pure knowledge of the Self as it really is.'

12. Training the Mind

There are not many people who can simply practise meditation on the Self, or on the Lord, aiming all the time at liberation, without becoming bored, or else being overwhelmed by waves of distraction, lassitude or fear. It is found that for most people there must be some encouragement, something tangible in everyday experience. So Patanjali in his Yoga Sutras gives six main means of practice for first purifying and then steadying the mind as it is, and for some of them he gives results by which progress can be checked. These results, however wonderful some of them may seem, are not liberation. But they mean a lightening of the present burden of living with nothing but a distant hope. They are ways of confirming at least something that the teacher and the tradition say. If some one thing, however little it may be, is confirmed, there is a surge of faith that the rest is true and confirmable also.

In a primitive country which suddenly became rich through discovery of minerals, the central government embarked on a programme of rapid education of the villagers. Young idealistic teachers were sent out from the capital to open schools in remote areas. One such teacher took with him a do-it-yourself radio construction set. His own set which he had meant to demonstrate was unfortunately badly broken during transit, but he showed the pupils photos of the people in the capital listening to the radio. They volunteered enthusiastically to help him build a set for the whole village to listen to. However after a few days the volunteers dropped off, and finally only one remained. It took a good time to finish the set, but in the end it was working and the villagers all thanked him. He asked some of the former volunteers, 'How was it that you lost interest? Didn't you believe me?' They replied, 'At first we believed you absolutely, but then it took so long, and what we were doing – joining up little wires and all the rest – seemed nothing to do with hearing music and plays which you promised us. It all began to seem impossible – that music should be coming through the air which no one could hear until we had joined up some bits of wire. In a way we still did believe you, but ... well, we sort of thought that perhaps it might work in the capital but not in our village!'

This experience made an impression on the teacher, and when he was ordered to a new village he took not only the do-it-yourself construction kit, but some compasses and magnets too. Before he talked about radio at all, he showed the villagers the compass needle, moved by an invisible and intangible force. He used the magnets to magnetise other pieces of metal, and gave some of the pupils these pieces to take home and play with. This time the volunteers did not fall away when they began making the radio; at times when he saw their faith was wavering, he said, 'The force we are preparing to harness in this set is the same which you have seen working in the compass and magnets.' Then their confidence revived.

Most minds are too disturbed to be able to meditate for long on the pure Self or the universal Self, and Patanjali gives seven classes of practice for purifying and steadying the mind. These easier practices are nearer to daily life and body-consciousness than the disciple feels that the universal Lord, or even the pure Self, can be. Without some practice on these lines, students tend to find the gap between the present state, darkened by passion and fear, and the absolute transcendence of the Self or the Lord, too great. Then they may give up.

Patanjali's practices are called collectively parikarman, which could be rendered as 'enriching'. Dr Shastri sometimes referred to it as refining the mind. The practices give results quickly – results which in the normal course may appear naturally, but in the higher stages of meditation; to experience one of them at the beginning gives confidence. For instance, a student who is particularly physically restless always turns out to be breathing irregularly. By practice on Om, his breathing will gradually become deep and slow naturally. But if he performs one of the breathing exercises consciously, he can remove the disturbance more quickly. Still, he has to remember what the aim is: to cure the restlessness, not to become expert in manipulating breath. To stop at one special practice, as if it were a sporting event, and abandon or postpone the jump beyond individuality into the universal, is to miss the point. It would correspond to playing with the magnets and refusing to build the radio. Sutra 30 of the first part of Patanjali's sutras lists nine main obstacles in the way of yoga, which distract the mind. They are, as explained by Shankara, *illness*; *rigidity* of mind; *doubt*, which is a notion – for instance, 'is that a post or a man?' – which touches both of two contradictory alternatives; *heedlessness*, being a lack of intensity (bhavana), not being constant in the practice for attaining samadhi; *slackness*, being lack of effort due to heaviness of body or mind; *attraction to the world*; *illusion* about the disciplines of yoga and the path; *failure to attain a stage* of samadhi; *instability*, which is a failure to remain steady in a meditation stage when it has been achieved. They are, says Shankara, distractions, adversaries, defects in yoga. They are above all distractions of the mind. It is clear that these correspond to some of the doshas of the Chapter of the

Self, and in both cases the recommendation is given to remove them by yoga practices.

Sutra 31 adds that they are generally evidenced by experience of pain, depression, restlessness of the body, and irregular breathing. Sutra 32 states that these obstacles can all be removed by practice on 'one principle', and Shankara remarks that this refers to some one out of the six parikarman practices.

But it has also been stated in Sutra 29 that the obstacles can be removed, and are removed, by meditation on the Lord by means of Om meditation practice. The Lord is described in Sutra 25, and Shankara makes his commentary on this the longest one in the whole work. It may be wondered why the parikarman practices are given at all, when the whole process can be effected by the Om practice alone. The length of Shankara's commentary on Sutra 25, which is mostly concerned with evidences for the existence of a supreme omniscient controlling Lord, gives a hint. Many would-be yogis are not convinced even intellectually about the matter, and in Shankara's time, those who performed religious rituals often regarded them more as magical ceremonies rather than worship. In fact one of the sects held that it is immaterial whether the gods exist or not. If the ceremonies are performed correctly, and the names of the gods pronounced, the results follow for the sacrificer. It was not his concern whether any deity exists corresponding to the name. The sacrificial priest of that sect regarded himself as somewhat like an electronics engineer today. The engineer knows what an electric charge will do to a wire, and the knowledge enables him to work effectively. As to what the charge is in itself, he leaves that to the philosophers – perhaps it is unanswerable.

But the position of the yogi is, that he wants to *know*. He is more like the physicists who first investigated electricity: they wanted to *know*, whether it was ultimately applicable in other fields or not. And the final conclusion of the yogi is, that happiness on this earth or in some heaven, as aimed at by the ritualists, is based on illusion. It depends on identification with body or mind, which in the end is an imprisonment. The physical body dies, the soul falls from heaven after its merits are exhausted, as the Chapter of the Self commentary says at the beginning. It is said in one of the accounts of heaven, that the soul suddenly becomes aware that its stay there is about to end, and that moment is a worse agony than any of the hells. Experience has shown, however, that few yogis can contemplate an immediate dis-identification from body and mind. The latent impressions of identity are too strong. They may try to imagine it, and think that they have an idea of it, but in fact it is not so. Children try to imagine themselves grown-up, but when they explain what they will do, it is nearly always some ridiculous exaggeration of what they are doing now.

So Patanjali gives the training meditations for those who cannot simply perform the Om practice in meditation on the Lord. The training meditations are nearer to the things of this world; they thin out the seed-bed of latent dynamic impressions called sanskaras, and then they steady the agitation of the mind. The sutras specify the results as prasadana and sthiti. The first means something like clearness: Dr Shastri also translates it as 'purification'. The second word means stability, firmness – it is in fact our English word 'steady'. These two things, clearness and steadiness, are the essential factors in yogic practice. First the mind is made a little clear, and then it becomes able to concentrate more and more steadily on subtle things; finally it can concentrate without flinching on the Lord and on the Self – it passes away into them, and that is liberation.

A merely pure mind, or temporarily steadied mind, do not necessarily lead to liberation. There are minds which are pure, but which merely enjoy the happiness of their sattva. They have no spirit of inquiry awake in them. There are other minds which are steady in pursuit of an objective like ambition, but because they are not clear, they are unable to free themselves from the fantasy even when it is ruining their lives.

The Patanjali sutras on parikarman are:

1.33 By intensification of friendliness towards the happy, compassion towards the suffering, goodwill towards virtue, overlooking sin, the mind becomes *clear*;

34 by either exhaling and checking the prana life-current,

35 or (by) mental perception of (divine) objects, the mind becomes *steady*;

36 or (by) the 'sorrowless radiant' (mental perception)

37 or (by) meditation on a mind free from passion,

38 or on the knowledge of dream and of dreamless sleep,

39 or on the Chosen Form.

40 Mastery is when mind can be steadied on anything from the ultimate in smallness to the ultimate in greatness.

13. The Four Feelings

The meditations on four feelings which are to be intensified through meditation are called bhavana: they are friendliness towards the happy, compassion for the suffering, goodwill towards virtue, and overlooking sin. Shankara in his commentary explains that these are meditations which must actualise themselves. Until the reactions in ordinary life have begun to modify themselves along the lines of the meditations, the cultivation of intensity has only begun.

Friendliness – maitri, a great word in Buddhism – is explained as a general gladness at the good fortune and happiness of another. The Mahatma Balarama Udasin, whom Dr Shastri knew and held in great regard, remarks that this friendliness must not be partisanship, what the world calls friendship. It has to be something like the friendliness of the Lord towards all beings – not taking the side of one against another. Shankara in his Gita commentary (to V. 29) stresses meditation on the Lord as the friend of all, who does good to them without expecting any return for it, and who lies in the hearts of all. Worldly friendship, on the other hand, is towards one person identified with body-mind, and involves hatred of those who are against him. The goodwill and friendliness of the world are often merely sentimentality, and do not do the good which is expected. A Chinese king heard a bull being driven to the temple for the annual sacrifice, and its melancholy bellow touched his heart; he felt that it somehow knew of what was to happen. He gave orders that the bull was to be returned and set free; 'sacrifice a ram instead', he told the minister. This was reported to the Confucian sage Mencius, who remarked that it was quite natural for the king to spare the bull and sacrifice a ram instead, because he had heard the bull, but not the ram. The king would be wrong, however, to suppose that he had done anything good. Similarly today some people are touched when they see a violent robber suffering in prison, and try to get him released; like the king, they see the robber but do not see the victims. 'The shepherd who is kind to wolves is cruel to sheep.' A modern teacher remarked of such cases that it is not reasonable to release the human being who finds himself caught in the wolf role. Those who feel a concern could do something to ameliorate the prison condition by personal visits and in other ways; and to put spiritual books into the prison library would be a service to both the prisoners and society.

In a sense, it is easier to feel goodwill towards the unhappy than towards the happy, because there is no question of envy. Those who are successful are generally targets of envy, their happiness being compared with the real or imagined sufferings of the others. It is a great meditation to fix the mind on happiness of others and realise it as a manifestation of the bliss aspect of Brahman. This is not nearly so easy as most people imagine; Iago was by no means an exceptional individual.

As the result of some good action in the past, beings have a momentary glimpse of the bliss which underlies all, but they think this glimpse is due just to the particular circumstances of the moment. The yogi is expected to take all experiences of happiness, in others as in himself, as a manifestation of truth, distorted to the degree to which the experiencer so arrogates the happiness to his individual self. To the yogi the happiness of others is a manifestation of the Krishna or attraction element of Brahman, and he feels friendliness towards it. This feeling has to be intensified by meditation and action.

Compassion towards suffering is the second of the four bhavana exercises. Bhavana in Sanskrit has the sense of saturating, steeping, completely infusing; psychologically it means something which permeates the whole mental life. The yogi exercises compassion in his thinking, in his meditation, and in his action which springs from them. He is expected to find skilful means for relieving suffering at its root, not superficially. To keep giving alcohol to a drunkard or money to a gambler whose vice is ruining his life and that of his family, is not compassion.

This is not to say that an enlightened man might not manage to use just that method. A Zen monk was asked to come and preach to a drunkard. 'I cannot do that,' he replied, 'but I will come and stay at the house for a week.' He told the family to go to bed early each evening, and himself used to produce some of the best quality rice-wine, which he would pour for his host. They stayed up talking late each night. At the end of the week the host said, 'I've enjoyed having you here – you're so cheerful and it has lightened my life. But it's surprising that you don't need any wine, because I'd thought no one could be really happy without it.' They said good-bye. Some weeks later the monk received a letter from the man saying that the drinking habit had been thrown off. It would be no use for an ordinary man to imitate such methods – the change was brought about by the spiritual light and strength within the monk, not by his outer actions.

Men of the world try to help suffering as their feelings dictate, supplemented with a little bit of reason, and perhaps tradition. But until there is a considerable power of meditation, it is often found that the acts do not have the expected results. Bhavana practice is meditation and practice of action together, not just meditation alone or action alone.

It is not creating a vague idea of compassion to all that suffers. This kind of practice can be depressing, because the yogi can be overwhelmed at the hopelessness of individual efforts to relieve what he sees as an ocean of suffering.

Nor is bhavana taking some pattern of action, like the parable of the Good Samaritan, and forcing oneself to follow it as a duty. This also leads to inner disturbance from the parts of the mind which are unconvinced. The English saying 'Cold as charity' is a cruel illustration.

One of the traditional methods of bhavana is to meditate for at least six weeks on an incident in the life of a saint or avatar till it becomes intensely vivid. It is as it were lived through. When doing this practice, an attempt must be made over the weeks and months to bring outer conduct into line with the theme of the incident, but not as a compulsory task without feeling.

As an example, this is how a yogi might be directed to make bhavana on the Good Samaritan story. (It would be distracting for a Westerner to take an unfamiliar story from an Eastern source, requiring many explanatory notes. Another advantage of a familiar story is to find out how deep the ordinary acquaintance with it has penetrated.) First he would learn this little story, just about 500 words, by heart. Even the dullest memory can do this in a week, by writing it on a card to carry round; at moments of waiting, some sentences of the story are recited internally, and when he sticks, he can glance at the card to get going again. If he uses the old translations, he should compare them once with a new one – the derisory 'two pence' of the Authorised Version means 'two silver pieces'. Here is the story, with its introduction, as it appears in the New English Bible (Luke 10:25):

On one occasion a lawyer came forward to put this test question to him: 'Master, what must I do to inherit eternal life?' Jesus said, 'What is written in the Law? What is your reading of it?' He replied, 'Love the Lord your God with all your heart, with all your soul, with all your strength, and with all your mind; and your neighbour as yourself.' 'That is the right answer,' said Jesus; 'do that and you will live.' But he wanted to vindicate himself, so he said to Jesus, 'And who is my neighbour?'

Jesus replied, 'A man was on his way from Jerusalem down to Jericho when he fell in with robbers, who stripped him, beat him, and went off leaving him half dead. It so happened that a priest was going down by the same road; but when he saw him, he went past on the other side. So too a Levite came to the place, and when he saw him went past on the other side. But a Samaritan who was making the journey came upon him, and when he saw him was moved to pity. He went up and bandaged his wounds, bathing them with oil and wine. Then he lifted him on to his own beast, brought him to an inn, and looked after him there. Next day he produced two silver pieces and gave them to the innkeeper, and said, 'Look after him; and if you spend any more, I will repay you on my way back.' Which of these three do you think was neighbour to the man who fell into the hands of the robbers?' He answered, 'The one who showed him kindness.' Jesus said, 'Go and do as he did.'

All the words of this story have to be examined, in the light of the New Testament as a whole, if the yogi knows it. Why is it a Samaritan? In the same gospel of Luke, Jesus calls a Samaritan whom he has cured 'this foreigner', remarking that the foreigner is more grateful than the Jews cured at the same time. In the gospel of John, Jesus is accused of being a Samaritan; elsewhere it is recorded that Jews will not associate with Samaritans, who are 'unclean'. A final point is, that when at the end the enquirer is asked, 'Which was neighbour to the man who had fallen into the hands of the robbers?' he does not make the natural reply, 'the Samaritan', but only says that he supposes it would be the merciful man. He cannot bring himself to utter the word 'Samaritan'. Why not?

To make bhavana on this story, the yogi first identifies himself with each character in turn. The victim is probably a pious Jew, who has just come from offering worship at the Temple in Jerusalem. Should not God have protected him? In each event of life, if it is meditated upon profoundly, the ultimate questions appear. He is attacked by robbers, who not merely take everything he has, but beat him and leave him for dead. This is not necessarily meaningless cruelty; the robbers do not want to leave a living man who could report on them, and recognise them. The victim lies helpless, half-conscious, on the side of the road. Anyone who has been beaten, or knocked into semi-consciousness, can revive his memory of that state for the bhavana; others can think back to a time when they were very ill, and vividly imagine what it would be like to have been thrown then on to the side of the road, naked and in great pain. The meditator lives through the experience of being picked up, gently bandaged, held on the ass and finally brought to an inn; the total collapse, the relief at being put to bed, then being looked after for several days; the wonder at finding that the benefactor has gone on without waiting for gratitude or any return.

The priest and the Levite (an assistant at the Temple) have had an undeserved reputation for extreme callousness. The man whom they saw was probably dead, and to have touched a dead body would have made them 'unclean' and ineligible to carry out their duties till they had undertaken ritual purification. Chapter 6 of the Book of Numbers explains the background – if someone died suddenly in the presence of a devotee engaged in a vow of purity, the devotee had to offer ritual sacrifice and then begin his period of the vow all over again, because he would have become unclean from mere accidental proximity to death. For bhavana it is essential not to look at the priest and Levite from the outside, but enter into the conflict of duties which was their situation.

As for the Samaritan himself, to identify with him may not be so easy as is generally imagined. This was entirely Jewish territory, and the victim must have been a hated Jew, probably on his way down from worshipping in the hated Temple. (Twenty years before, the Samaritans had deliberately defiled the Temple, and their own temple on Mount Gerizim was still in ruins after its destruction by the Jewish king Hyrcanus over a century before.) The yogi in his bhavana lives through vividly the details of washing and binding the wounds, and when the man revives a little, supporting him on the ass to the inn. The Samaritan knows he is despised by the Jew as unclean. The next day, having seen the injured man a little better, the Samaritan goes; he evidently knows the innkeeper well, and makes provision for the victim's full recovery. But he himself goes, without hanging about for any gratitude. This is a theme which recurs constantly in Christ's teaching; it is the theme of the Bhagavad Gita on action: 'Do right action without any attachment to results.'

Both the Gita and the New Testament stress that the man who does charity, expecting and receiving appreciation for it, is a good man, but he is not the highest type of man. In the Gita this charity is said to be mixed with the guna rajas, passion-struggle; Christ says simply that they have their reward – from men.

There are other meanings in the fact that the Samaritan passed on without waiting.

The further form of the bhavana is to picture Christ telling this parable, the yogi being one of those who hear him. He now lives through each part as the story is told – and yet is aware of the teller all the time.

When this happens, the story begins to take on its own life; it becomes radiant, as Patanjali says. Some of the details reveal a new meaning, not merely intellectually but in feeling, and ultimately a meaning deeper than either thinking or feeling. For instance, the phrase 'and your neighbour as your Self' can begin to unfold itself. Humanists who reduce Christianity to a system of ethics fail to understand this phrase, partly because they ignore the 'love the Lord' which precedes it, and which also comes from the Old Testament. It is not noticed that Jesus gave his approval 'that is the right answer' to the combination of the two phrases which the lawyer, who must have been a learned and spiritual man, had extracted from Leviticus and Deuteronomy, and put together as a summary of the Law.

When the bhavana begins to enter sometimes into samadhi, the story extends. The robbers themselves are victims of other robbers – greed and cruelty have stripped them of their spiritual discrimination and power of love. Who is the Samaritan who will rescue the victims of the spiritual robbers? How will it be done?

The world itself is a victim of the robber of cosmic ignorance. The whole universe becomes wrapped up in the parable of the Good Samaritan, told by Christ to an expert in the Law. The parable becomes externalised to the limit of greatness, and also it becomes internalised. In the soul of man are the robbers, the victim, the ones who pass by on the other side, the Samaritan, and the innkeeper.

Goodwill towards virtue is a great spiritual quality, and it is placed very high because the human mind feels such relief at pulling down something felt to be greater than itself. In the list of doshas in the Chapter of the Self, spite, false speech, and backbiting all have reference to the vice of jealousy listed after them. Perhaps this vice is pointed out so frequently in the yogic classics because it is difficult to recognise in oneself. At the time of the French Revolution, parents were recommended to give their new-born children personal names representing the ideals of the Revolution, like Fraternity, instead of the names of Christian saints as hitherto. But the directive had to be changed, because some parents began giving names like 'Death to the Aristocrats' to their children, showing clearly what the so-called ideals of liberty and equality stood for in the minds of some of their supporters.

The judicial murders of Socrates and Christ are well known; Buddha's relative Devadatta made repeated attempts to kill him, St John of the Cross narrowly escaped murder by monks of his order, attempts were made to kill Mohammad and George Fox. Dr Shastri sometimes quoted an Indian saying, 'Do good and be abused for it'; there is a humorous version of it, 'Do good and ... run!'

In the yogic view, all great qualities are of divine origin: 'Know Me ... I am the intelligence of the intelligent, the bravery of the brave, the energy of the mighty workers, devoid of passion and attachment; in all beings I am the desire not opposed to righteousness.' The yogi is to think, and meditate until it becomes a conviction, that a virtue is not the property of the one now manifesting it. In fact, virtue is not true virtue while it is fully conscious; when it becomes unconscious, a natural expression, it is real virtue. 'Let not the right hand know what the left hand is doing,' says Christ.

Overlooking or disregarding sin is the last of the four practices in this group. Shankara explains it as having as little to do with sinful people as possible during the training period. This is a negative practice, and it may be asked why it is mentioned as a 'refinement' of the mind. He says:

> If it were not mentioned, the mind would go to association even with people who are habitually unrighteous. From the taint which arises from having dealings with them, the mind would become unfit for the practice of Friendliness and the others. Let not sin arise in oneself from engaging in undertakings which depend on habitual wrong-doing. This is why indifference is mentioned in this context.

Disregard of sin does not mean standing aside from the suffering of a victim. But it does mean to be free from the mixture of self-righteousness and animal fear and rage which calls itself 'indignation'. And yet, how can anyone think of, not to say witness, the cruelties of a Nero or a Stalin without indignation? In the yogic analysis, these things are on the level of a cat torturing a mouse; the human being saves the mouse from the cat if he can, but does not hate the cat because he knows this is its nature. Tyrants great or small often function on the cat level. Small boys are sometimes cruel from the adult standpoint; they pull the wings off flies and laugh at their struggles. They have not the imagination to feel into the suffering they create. The parent knows that it has to stop, but he does not hate the child.

Indignation is caused by fear, a threat to security. Until a yogi has had a glimpse of immortality, he will be subject to fear and consequently to this kind of indignation. He has to treat it as a tapas, and try to pass through it without losing his interior balance for too long. He can reckon his progress by finding how quickly he recovers. With some people a shock can frighten and depress for weeks, sometimes for a lifetime. Those who practise yoga find that after only a few days, something rises within them that can throw off the depression. If they continue with Yogic practice, and especially Om practice, they find that as soon as the immediate pressure is over, an inner strength rises and revives their spirits. Finally even during the time of stress, an inner support is felt.

Indignation is an impulse of rajas, generally rising as a reaction to fear, which is of tamas. Rajas is better than tamas – it is better to feel indignation than to be paralysed by fear. But rajas must be transcended. An opponent must sometimes be vigorously resisted, but that resistance should be like battling against a force of nature, for instance a storm. We do not personify the storm, nor do we hate it even when fighting for life.

In his commentary on the Gita, Madhusudana discusses the Four Feelings or bhavanas as cultivated in the yoga of Patanjali, and explains that the practice will first weaken and then destroy the latent drives of Passion in the seed-bed which is at the root of the mind. Shankara in his commentary explains the word 'bhavana' as 'causing something to be'. As already pointed out, it has also the sense of soaking, permeating. The concept is different from conventional morality, where frustrated instincts still boil under a veneer of control. Bhavana can and must change the very roots of the mind, and this is possible because in the yogic psychology drives like power and sex are not the essential nature of the human being, but are based on 'illusory notions', as the Chapter of the Self commentary says.

Some Western psychology, like the early Chinese philosopher Kao-tsu, tends towards a pessimistic conclusion, because it is thought that truth and virtue are things acquired. Thinkers of this persuasion have argued that drives like hunger, power and sex are fundamental; they may be distorted, even sublimated apparently completely, but at a deep level they are always crying for satisfaction. In the yogic psychology, these things are not fundamental, but superimposed notions of difference on a fundamental divinity which is a unity in everything. 'He who is constant in all beings, wise, immortal, firm ... The seer meditating, seeing everything in the Self, will not be deluded; and whoever sees the Self alone in everything, he is Brahman, glorious in the highest heaven.' The Gita makes this vision the whole basis of true morality:

> He sees who sees the supreme Lord abiding in all beings,
> The undying in the dying;
> Seeing the same Lord established in all,
> He harms not the Self by the Self, and attains the highest.

This is the same basis of morality as in the quotation from Leviticus cited by the teacher of the Law to Christ, 'thou shalt love thy neighbour as thy Self: I the Lord.' Christ extended the notion of neighbour to include all.

In the third part of the Patanjali yoga sutras, it states that when the bhavanas on friendliness and the others enter the state of samadhi, there come 'powers'. One of the commentaries explains that one of the powers is that friendliness and compassion are aroused in others. These powers may come when the yogi's meditation on, say, compassion has reached samadhi – that is to say the meditator disappears, and the meditation process disappears, and only compassion is there, becoming radiant. It is not a human, feeling compassion and giving expression to it; it is Compassion, making use of that body and mind to express itself. At this time there is no individual choosing or calculating about individual welfare. It is only compassion incarnate, and actions are not centred round the individual at all – hence they can be much more free. Here are two examples.

The general had smashed the rebel army, and proposed to execute their leaders at a big public occasion the next morning. After that, he thought he would go to see the flowers at the Peony Temple. The monks there grew tree-peonies as a contribution to the beauty of the neighbourhood; when the flowers bloomed, many visitors came to see the hundreds of flowers. The general therefore sent a messenger to tell the head priest that he would visit the temple the next afternoon, after the executions. The priest, who was a fully realised yogi of the Mantra Sect, said to the messenger, 'Come round with me and look at the flowers.' On the way he picked up a little sickle. As they passed each tree, the priest cut off the flowers. The messenger was aghast, but too bewildered to say anything. When they had gone right round the gardens, the priest faced the messenger and said, 'Tell him I've murdered them.'

The messenger returned and told his tale. The general's eyes grew red with anger, but then he became thoughtful. The rebel leaders were sent back to their own people.

A duke was displeased with one of his ministers who had disobeyed him. He sentenced the minister to die at the end of the month. One of the court counsellors, who practised a certain form of yoga, argued against the sentence. 'He has made a mistake, but remember that he served you loyally for a long time before that.' The duke heard him out, but met all his arguments by referring to the clear words of the law which laid down the death penalty for this offence. When the counsellor persisted, the duke cut him short: 'I am the highest judge in this dukedom. I have heard your reasons and met them, and told you my decision. If you still persist in presenting reasons, you are as good as saying that my decision is unjust. That would be treason.' The counsellor was silent. Next morning he presented himself again, and asked for mercy for the minister. 'And what are your reasons?' asked the duke smoothly. 'I have no reasons,' replied the counsellor, 'I just ask for mercy for him.' The duke shouted, 'Get out!' Next day it was the same – 'No special reasons.' The duke irritably ordered him to be punished. Next day the counsellor appeared again – 'No special reasons.' The duke was impressed and pardoned the minister.

On reading such stories, there is bound to be a feeling that it is a question of being able to say certain lines, like an actor, and if they are well said, then the other party also will say his lines and all will be well. The Archbishop of Canterbury under William the Conqueror was an Italian, Lanfranc, and he relates an interesting story of his youth. He had read how a saint in Lombardy had been invited to visit a rich man's family, and the rich man had sent him a horse on which to make the journey. However, as he was passing through a forest, he was set on by an outlaw who knocked him off the horse and rode off with it. The whip was left lying on the ground, and the saint picked it up and ran after the outlaw, calling to him, 'Take the whip too – you will need it when you come to the river!'

As it happened, when Lanfranc was travelling in France to Cluny, he himself was set on in the same way, and the robber stripped him of everything except his cloak and went off. Lanfranc remembered the story of the Lombard saint, and its happy ending, and went after the robber. When he caught him up he offered him the cloak too. Lanfranc remarks, 'He thought I was mocking him, and he beat me until I was nearly killed. And that was right, for that saint in Lombardy had given that the robber might take, but I was giving in the hope that he might be converted and give me back everything he had taken!'

And furthermore, the powers arising from samadhi may not necessarily preserve the individual life of the yogi. That life is only one element in the universe; the manifestation of Compassion may not include preserving that particular life. In fact the counsellor of the duke, mentioned above, was executed by that duke's successor for a very similar protest.

There are other powers which can arise from bhavana on friendliness and the others. But Shankara remarks, in his commentary on sutra III.23, that though the man of bhavana is a 'powerful' man, if he concentrates on any of the supernormal powers in the world he invites a recurrence of Ignorance. For example, if a yogi were to concentrate on achieving telepathic power, he would achieve it, but it would involve polluting his partially purified mind with the thoughts of passion of an unpurified mind, and that would set him back in his yoga. Shankara is definite that such powers exist – he says in his Brahma-sutra commentary that they are a fact, which cannot be brushed aside merely by an emphatic denial. But to concentrate on them invites a darkening of the mind.

Sometimes this darkening may not be apparent to the man himself. An adhyatma yogi fell in with a magician travelling the same path, and the magician said to him, 'Your yoga is only words. At the end you are only what you were before. You speak of removing limitations, but you cannot do it. Now in our path we do actually remove limitations; we extend our powers.' 'But you do not remove the limitation of individuality,' said the yogi, 'and while that remains, though you may think you remove some physical limitations, others will be imposed on you, perhaps unconsciously.' 'If they are unconscious, what would it matter?' retorted the magician. 'Anyhow, we shall see.'

They came to a river and could not see any boat. The magician stood on the bank, muttering certain syllables again and again. His body began to tremble and his aspect changed; he looked as light as a feather. He threw his straw hat on the water, and stepped on it. Spreading the sleeves of his cloak like a sail, he was carried across the river by a breeze which had sprung up from nowhere. The yogi called a farewell which was ignored.

After a little time, a boat came down the river and the yogi hailed it; the boatman amiably took him across the river for a little fee. On the other side the magician was waiting for him, and as he stepped ashore said triumphantly, '*Now* do you see the superiority of our path! You had to wait while I crossed directly.'

'Yet here we are together,' remarked the yogi.

'What do you mean?'

'Why, your magic made you light, and so you crossed the river and you were ahead of me. But when you had crossed, something made you heavy, and you could not move till I came up. You had to wait so that you could score off me. Surely there is no loosening of the limitations by such things.'

It may reasonably be asked, 'If these powers are no help in yoga, and are not to be pursued, why are they mentioned at all?' One reason is that when meditation and worship are being practised, sometimes one of these things momentarily manifests itself spontaneously. If the yogi has not been warned of it, he may go nearly mad with excitement; he may think that the tradition he is being taught knows nothing of what is now happening, and is merely theoretical. *This*, he may feel, is something actual and definite, whereas the rest was merely big words. His excitement inflates his individuality and rouses the passion for power; this darkens the instrument, which in the end no longer manifests anything unusual. At first he deceives himself, but later when he finds it has gone for ever, he may fall into bitterness and despair.

George Fox had many such experiences, but he never attributed them to himself. When a mob came to lynch him at Cambridge, they fell back before a light which they saw coming from him; yet soon afterwards in the same year he was badly beaten and stoned. Fox carefully collected a number of such cases from his own experience and those of other Quakers, and made a book of them; but this was suppressed by his literary executors and has disappeared, though some of the main incidents have been reconstructed from references elsewhere. Fox believed that such manifestations of the Lord's power were a great aid to faith, but he never relied on them, and never prayed to receive them.

Shankara's view was similar; he says that one or two experiences are a great help for a beginner, as an encouragement; but if he prizes them for themselves, they prevent further progress.

The difference between exercising such powers of the mind and exercising ordinary powers of applied science is that with science the motive does not affect the instrument, whereas in the powers that may come through yoga, the mind is itself the instrument, and an individual motive affects it detrimentally. Then they become unreliable and finally cease. Repeatedly in his commentary Shankara says that these are among the most subtle bonds which tie the self to individuality; like the other bonds, they are cut by yoga practice based on truth, and especially by the Om practice. The truth is that individual self-existence, whether felt to be weak or felt to be semi-divine, is an illusion.

14. Pranayama

Sutra 1.34 By either exhaling and checking the prana life-current

Prana cannot be translated exactly into present-day English; the original sense of 'spirit' might come close to it. Control of prana is not the same as control of the breath, but one of the movements of prana is in phase with breathing, and the prana movement is most easily perceived by trying to become aware of it along with movement of breath.

Control of prana, or pranayama, is introduced after the bhavana meditations on friendliness and the others, but most of the commentators agree that this is not an alternative to them. The Mahatma Balarama points out that Sutra 55 gives the friendliness meditations as a means of making the mind *clear*, whereas this one and the ones following it refer to making the mind *steady*. Both transparency of mind *and* steadiness are necessary for samadhi. Here is what he says:

It cannot be right that by *any* of these alternatives purification of the mind is brought about, for mere expulsion and restraining of prana could never produce refining of the mind. It is steadiness of mind that may be attained by expulsion and restraint of prana, as one alternative; and pranayama and the following alternatives are optional means of attaining steadiness. But pranayama is not a means for making the mind pure. That this is the right way to understand it is shown by what the Lord says in the Gita, 'In a refined mind, buddhi quickly becomes steady', and there is also what holy Vyasa has said, 'When mind has been refined, its concentration attains stability.' This makes it clear that without making the mind pure, it will hardly be made steady. Thus expulsion and restraint of prana are presented by the sutras as a means of steadying a mind which has already been purified by meditation on friendliness and the others, and control of prana is not by itself a means of making the mind pure.

The practices (friendliness, expulsion of prana, etc.) are not optional alternatives; nor are their results (refinement of mind, and its steadiness) optional alternatives. The meditations on friendliness etc., which are the means to refinement of the mind, must always be combined (with at least one of the other methods given) to attain steadiness. So the conclusion is: no option in regard to meditations on friendliness etc., which must always be practised.

Shankara, however, in his commentary states that meditation on friendliness, etc. can also give stability of mind in addition to making it clear. This is in accord with the importance which in his Gita commentary he gives to the meditation on the Lord as the friend of all. He remarks also that the other methods for steadying the mind, such as pranayama, are appropriate depending on the person and the time and the place.

In the exercises in pranayama, the yogi tries to become aware of pranic currents by visualising or feeling that the breath itself is moving along the pranic channels. Then gradually, or quickly in some cases, he begins to notice a current which moves at the same rhythm as the breath, but is not the same as the physical breath. This current is called prana (sometimes divided into five according to its movement), though in classical texts it is still often referred to as 'air' or 'breath', and it is assumed that the reader will understand it as prana.

Sutra 34 speaks of exhaling and restraining prana, and Shankara explains this as two separate practices. The first consists of lengthening the out-breath; in actual practice it is done with a series of long Oms, each one of which is gradually extended to fifteen seconds or longer.

The yoga sutras are in analytical form, and different elements are presented in isolation. But in training there is generally a combination. Pranayama is a very ancient practice, and when Manu praises it so highly (the present text of his Law-book dates from only about A.D. 500 but parts of it are known to go back for several centuries before that) he speaks of it in conjunction with Om. So also Yajnavalkya explains that pranayama in its highest form is 'seeded' – which means that it has the 'seed-syllable' Om combined with it.

The repetition of Om, sounding it very quietly but audibly on long exhalations, is pranayama of the first form; with practice the yogi begins to feel a vibration in his body, which means that he is becoming aware of the pranic current. He also feels that his body is becoming filled with light; this is a well-known effect which has great significance for the progress of meditation. Swami Rama Tirtha, himself a scientist, says of this:

> For one minute, cast overboard all desire; chant Om; no attachment, no repulsion, perfect poise, and there your whole being is light personified ... While you are chanting Om, feel that you are Light, Glory. Light you are. Christ said, 'I am the light of the world.' Mohammad and all the great saints spoke in the same way ... It is just as much a matter of experience as any experiment performed in any laboratory.

From merely making the expirations very long, fine and slow, the mind becomes steady. But unless one is also practising the friendliness bhavana, or some other practice like Om, the mind will indeed become steadied by the pranayama but afterwards there will be a reaction. The invigoration produced by pranayama creates an excitement, and the power-instinct or some other passion may rise with great force. But if he has practised with the Om syllable, feeling it as the expressing-sound of the Lord, he will not be subject to these disturbances so much, and if they do come, he will be able to detach himself from them. Om repetition removes the obstacles, as Sutra 29 has declared.

The second pranayama practice referred to in the sutra is 'checking' or 'restraining' prana. Shankara gives this as a separate practice, and it is a full course of controlling inspiration and expiration, and holding the breath. This is a much more elaborate process, and it involves many restrictions. There must be absolute abstinence from sex, from talking or walking much, from over-eating, and from eating at all anything acid, astringent, pungent, salt, or bitter, and he must live in retirement in a little hut. The movement of the pranic currents is very fine, and unless the physical condition is brought to a state of extreme sensitivity and balance, they cannot be discerned. By practice the breath becomes longer and finer, and it can be held for longer and longer as the body becomes adapted.

One main purpose of all these operations is what is technically called 'udghata' or up-stroke. It is explained by Shankara that the 'air' (prana) which has been excited and then controlled, rises abruptly from the abdomen to the head. Vachaspati and later commentators explain that the current is felt moving abruptly from the navel to the head. It can be like a shock, or a sensation of inner light moving up and producing sometimes a feeling like a giddiness. This is the first 'up-stroke'. The yogi notes how many breaths it has taken him in the practice that day to produce the up-stroke.

The current does not remain in the head, but it can produce an exhilaration which lasts a good time. One purpose of mentioning these things is not to recommend them, but because they can occur spontaneously even in a yogi not practising pranayama, and he must be able to recognise what has happened. It has to be expected in some cases that the general invigoration will lead to a strengthening of instinctive impulses. Unless the yogi is prepared to increase correspondingly his practice of tapas (austerity), svadhyaya (study and repetition of Om), and worship of the Lord, his yogic career may be cut short for quite a time. To practise pranayama without observing the disciplines, particularly sexual abstinence, can lead to an increase of obstacles, especially trembling of the body which can become uncontrollable.

In general, teachers recommend pranayama to disciples of bulky build, rather than to nervous people who are thin.

Swami Rama Tirtha did not recommend anyone to practise the second form of pranayama; he said that it was unnecessarily complicated and dangerous, and that the 'up-stroke' could be achieved in a much more natural way, without complications:

Meditate on the meaning of Om. With language, lips, feeling, action, affirm it. Chant Om with every fibre of your body. Begin with little force; sound first comes from throat, then chest, lower and lower down until from base of spine; then electric shock, opening of Sushumna, your breathing becomes rhythmical, all germs of disease leave you ...

About opening Sushumna, about the thousand-petalled Lotus, waste not your time; all will come to you. Do not confuse yourself with meandering zigzag paths, or you will have to repent.

15. The Self-terminating Experiences

Yogic practices for preparing the mind for knowledge are not necessarily concerned with ultimate truth, but may be just to purify and steady the mind as it now stands, with all its present preconceptions.

It is found that in many cases there has to be some definite experience, however small, of something beyond the normal range. Unless this happens, everything is merely theoretical, and the highest Self seems so remote that yogic aspirants give up in despair. So certain practices may be given to steady the faith of the pupil, as well as his mind. Sutra 1.35 refers to a set of five of them:

or (by) mental perception of (divine) objects, the mind becomes steady

Shankara in his commentary on this gives examples of what are called dharana. The word means to support or maintain, and the practices consist in fixing the attention on to one place. He adds that before this practice can be undertaken successfully the yogi must be living a self-controlled life of extreme independence, practising some austerity, studying the scriptures, and worshipping God. He must also know how to seat himself upright and still, in balance and at ease, for a long time.

Now he fixes his attention on the nose. Many yogis, in India and outside, direct the gaze on to the tip of the nose; it is found by experience that if the pupils of the eyes are controlled, a bridle is put on the mind. There is a knack of doing this without strain, which can be acquired without too much difficulty. At first it feels unnatural, and some people feel that it makes the forehead ache. If so, they should stop, rub some oil on the forehead, and begin again. Practice of ten minutes morning and evening for six weeks generally gives mastery of the technique. Shankara says that the yogi should be aware of his sense of smell vividly.

After practice of some time which varies with the individual, but is generally something like six weeks, the yogi experiences first a little, and then continuously, a delightful fragrance, which is just like the normal sense-functioning but much more intense and varied.

Shankara explains that yoga drives towards face-to-face experience, and a first experience like this creates enthusiasm for the practice of yoga. The fragrance gives joy because it awakens confidence in the whole yoga system, and in the tradition which has given the practice and predicted the result. It is given so that a student may confirm one thing early on in his career, in his own living experience. Until something definite has happened, everything taught, right up to the final doctrines of Self-realisation and liberation, is all as it were merely taken second-hand; from time to time doubts are likely to arise as to whether after all it is true or not.

'Until some one thing has been directly perceived by one's own sense, the higher mind (buddhi) is likely sometimes to waver.' But after one direct experience, however small, it is reasonable to suppose that the rest can be confirmed also. However, Shankara makes the point that this sort of experience has no spiritual value in itself; it is not to be lingered over. He compares it to the smoke which appears when a man is making fire in the traditional way, by pressing a stick into another and twirling the first one rapidly. The friction produces heat which first shows itself as smoke.

Smoke is not at all what is wanted, and to stop at smoke, however fragrant it might be, would make the whole process meaningless. Moreover when the man stops, even the smoke soon disappears.

Shankara does not discuss this practice of perceiving divine fragrance any further; he regards it as a practice which can be dispensed with. In his commentary on a parallel passage in the Svetasvatara Upanishad, he remarks that the practice is 'inferior'. He does not even bother to outline the other practices of this set of five, namely perceiving divine colours, tastes, touch, and sound. He believes that the perception of light, as described in the next sutra, is a far better basis of practice. This will be set out a little later, but there are one or two points still to be made about the 'sense' experiences.

They are not like what the yogi may imagine beforehand; all the accounts show a sort of surprise when the experiences first come. They are more beautiful than anything in the world, and are quite different from hallucinations or dreams. The commentators say that they are genuine perceptions, but of objects not normally accessible to perception. If they produce attachment to their delight, it blocks further progress in yoga, because independence is lost. After a few such experiences, the teacher always directs the pupil to meditations on truth. Attachment to these higher sense experiences, like any attachment, darkens and restricts the mind, which loses its purity and strength.

They come and go. They are self-terminating, because the excitement they arouse interferes with the necessary concentration, which becomes split between the meditation, and what he expects to get as a result. The same applies to drug experiences.

There is a traditional story on the point. A yogi who lived on top of a hill in a remote area used to meditate every day either inside his little hut or in front of the door, just as the impulse took him. A poisonous snake which lived in the roots of a nearby tree came to know the man, and feeling some sort of attraction to him, used to coil itself round his neck when he was motionless in meditation. The yogi became aware of it but did not mind; as he slowly came out of meditation the snake would quietly go back to its own home.

The villagers in the valley used to send one of their number to take some milk and rice to the yogi every day. Once the messenger saw the snake coiled round his neck. In this village they were worshippers of the god Shiva, who is classically represented with snakes round his neck, symbolising tamed passions. The villager fell down and worshipped the yogi as Shiva. Next day another messenger saw the same thing. A few days later, the headman brought the rice; he waited till the yogi came out of meditation and the snake had gone, and then asked whether the whole village could come to see it.

The yogi agreed, but said, 'You must not disturb the snake. So stand a good distance off. I will meditate in front of the hut tomorrow, so that you will be able to see.' The next day he sat in meditation as usual, while the villagers stood some way off to see the miracle. But the snake never again came to the yogi.

16. The Light Experiences

Sutra 1.36 or (by) the sorrowless radiant (mental perception)

Shankara explains this as a much more important practice, and many teachers make it the first step, omitting the previous ones. The centre of attention (dharana) is the 'heart centre', roughly where the ribs meet. Some yogis put a dab of sandal paste there before sitting; the fragrance rising helps them to keep attention centred. Two hours is not too long for the practice, says the teacher Swami Mangalnath in the *Heart of the Eastern Mystical Teaching*.

When the yogi can hold attention steadily at that spot, he generally becomes aware of something like a lotus, made of light, and he meditates on it. Many Westerners have only a hazy idea of what a lotus looks like, having only seen them from a distance. Like many of these traditional similes, this one has been chosen carefully to give an idea of the experience, but there is no necessity to stick absolutely to it. In some traditions it is spoken of as a shallow bowl, and there are other illustrations also. It is not a question of auto-suggesting a particular form, but of having enough idea to be able to recognise the experience when it comes. It will never be exactly like the anticipation.

When the 'lotus' perception is familiar, he is told to meditate on a light shining in it. As an indication, it is said to be like a flame, traditionally the size of his own thumb. If he is a devotee of an incarnation, he can meditate on the standing form of that incarnation, made up of light. But the form must be very familiar to him before he will be able to do it.

Sometimes a teacher directs meditation on the sun, or the moon, or a ray of light, or a jewel. All this is still dharana – the yogi comes to feel that there is at his heart centre, in another set of dimensions as it were, a great space like a clear sky, and in that sky shining the sun or moon or a gem. He does not yet feel that he *is* these things, because the meditation has not yet come to samadhi, but he sees them. The commentators add that they are true objects, as real, and also as illusory, as the things of ordinary experience.

Shankara says in his commentary that if the yogi simply keeps attention on the heart centre, he becomes aware of the lotus there, and then there comes gradually awareness of the nature of mind as it really is.

What is the buddhi in its nature? It is resplendent, always shining, like shining space pervading all. When one is concentrating simply on the heart lotus, but there is still some unsteadiness in the buddhi, so that the natural likeness of it to the purity of Atman has not yet been attained, then this radiant experience becomes manifested as appearances of sun, moon, or a precious gem and so on. When (in time) the buddhi comes to samadhi on 'I Am', and then does attain its natural likeness to the Self, it becomes waveless like the great sea, peaceful, infinite, 'I Am' alone.

The teacher often gives one of the radiant forms as a meditation, partly because if he says nothing, the pupil may be disconcerted or excited when it comes. If one is taken as the object of meditation, the preliminary light appearance will tend to be in that form, though really it is all-pervading. When in the winter they cut through the ice on the lake to get water, it always first appears in the form of the cut – whether a circle, a triangle, a square and so on. It must first appear in some limited form, though it is everywhere under the ice. In the same way, the infinite ocean of light, also described as an infinite shining space, first appears in a form corresponding roughly (but not altogether) to the 'set' of the pupil's mind, consciously or unconsciously determined.

The light perception is like the perception of fragrance in that it gives confidence and faith in the yoga. It is true that unusual perceptions of fragrance or light would not necessarily convince a nervously critical mind; in such cases there may have to be experience of something like pre-cognition, of some unlikely event that duly happens. Wang Yang-ming, the last of the great Confucian sages, records such experiences during a period of seclusion in meditation. They were later confirmed by events, but he remarks that it was only playing with the powers of the mind, and did not lead to any spiritual progress at all.

These pre-cognitive experiences too are self-terminating; the excitement invariably dissipates the necessary calm of mind. And those whose extreme scepticism is based on a deep hidden fear may still persuade themselves that their memory must have been at fault.

The commentator is right when he points out that yoga cannot be practised indefinitely on a basis of 'hypothetical probability'; it cannot be kept up without real faith. If a yogi does practise on the traditional lines, he gets enough experience to convince a sensible man. If his intellect still complains that no proof is ever final, he must turn to look at how much proof he requires for the convictions on which his ordinary life is based. It is always found that he is guilty of a psychological fallacy, which has been called the Fallacy of Fluctuating Rigour. This demands an impossibly high degree of confirmation for what one wants to avoid, while perfectly satisfied with much less for what one emotionally accepts. Such a man does not get far at yoga, or indeed anything else as a rule.

Ultimately the real confirmations are changes in consciousness, expressed in outer life as inspiration, supported by whatever energy and courage may be necessary to implement it.

The practice of perceiving light at the heart centre need not terminate itself, because it can lead on to samadhi, when the meditator and object of meditation become one. The yogi no longer feels the radiance as separate, with himself aware of it (excited by the experience). He feels that he *is* the radiance, that his buddhi has become pure, waveless like a great sea of light, serene, infinite, 'I-am' alone. This is still a mental experience but it is one of the highest possible. The mind has become very like the Self in purity. Such experiences are reported in the Upanishads, and in the descriptions of yoga practice in the Mahabharata.

As a result of the practice of any of the means taught in this sutra or the last, some one portion of the yoga practice having been made a matter of direct perception, doubt having been thus dispelled and faith established firmly in the teachings about subtle things right up to liberation, the flow of extravertive mental functions is pacified, and the highest detachment is accomplished.

In his Hokyoki account of training in early thirteenth-century China, Dogen, one of the greatest Japanese Zen masters, mentions the 'fragrant' and other effects. His teacher said to him: 'I see you in the training hall sitting in meditation in the day and at night without falling asleep, and that is very good. After a time, you are sure to experience an exquisite fragrance, to which no worldly one can compare, and this is a favourable sign. Another favourable sign is to see before you something like a slow rain falling. Again if there arise various sensations of touch, this is also a good sign.' But these were only to be taken as signs, and the teacher added that he must push further along the path of meditation as urgently 'as if you were shaking something burning off your head'.

There are also mentions in the English medieval *Cloud of Unknowing*, with a strong admonition not to remain stuck in such experiences. This is the same warning as that given by Shankara.

He says that there are four classes of yogi, and the first is a man who has had one of these direct experiences, preferably the 'radiant'. Till then he is not classed as a yogi at all. Shankara remarks that the radiant perception is the real one, with the others merely preliminary. For some people, however, they are easier. Shankara mentions that the life must be self-controlled and independent, and the yogi must be studying the scriptures, repeating Om, and worshipping God. His warning about detachment comes again and again in his commentary on the yogas. To become dependent on any mental experience, however elevating it may be, is to be in a prison. Even if the bars are of gold, and the view through them beautiful, and the food luxurious, the cell is cramped and it is still a prison.

17. Passionlessness

Sutra 1.37 or (by) meditation on a mind free from passion

Some commentators explain the practice as meditation, ultimately with a sense of identity, on some saint who is free from passion. One way is to live through incidents in his life vividly through meditation.

Shankara gives a different practice, which is to consider the idea of 'freedom from passion', and he instances a well-known Indian example, how even the most passionate man feels his lust subside in the presence of one woman, namely his mother. There are other examples; one given by Dr Shastri was that there are certain fruits in the Himalayas which have a very attractive appearance, and the hungry pilgrim finds his mouth watering as he sees them. But when the guide explains how poisonous they are, the desire disappears. Their beauty is still appreciated, but the desire to eat them has gone.

The examples show that passion is not something inevitable; in these cases it disappears, though not forcibly repressed. If it can disappear on these occasions, then in principle it can disappear on others also.

18. Dream and Sleep

Sutra 1.38 or on the knowledge of dream and of (dreamless) sleep

One commentator understands the first part of this sutra as meaning that when a man awakens from a dream of a god, he should remain as long as possible in the memory of that dream; the dreamless sleep he understands as the sleep of a man in whom the doshas are very attenuated. These meditations, made on awakening, are thought to give knowledge.

Shankara, however, though he does not necessarily deny such an interpretation, takes it to mean meditating on the subtle analysis of dream and sleep. 'Knowledge of dream' does not mean knowledge of any object in a dream; the mind meditates on its own essence, by means of consideration of dream. The yogi is to meditate on knowledge as it is in itself, apart from any objects. Knowledge in itself is illumination, and he is to meditate on the true nature of knowledge, but not on remembered dream objects, because that would involve being implicated in them. Deep sleep consists of non-perception of any individual thing, and the meditation is on the idea of non-existence, namely peaceful, infinite, experienced, and unmoving. It is natural, concludes Shankara, that steadiness of the mind should come about by these meditations on dream and sleep.

To perform them requires a good deal of careful analysis first. The points are elaborately discussed in some of Shankara's other commentaries, but here he just refers to them, and the arguments can only be outlined. In dream, there is a light. What is the light under which the objects of the dream are seen? It may be said that it is the memory of the sun and so on, but a memory is not a light. What is the light which brings the memory-impressions to clear manifestation as dream-objects? To do this meditation the yogi sits in a stable posture, closes his eyes, and allows the mind to make pictures. Then he tries to isolate the light under which the pictures are known. In the case of dreamless sleep, a crucial point in Shankara's philosophy is that consciousness is not dissolved along with the sense-impressions and thoughts. In ordinary experience it is not distinguished from them. It is accepted by the yogis that in dreamless sleep there is no perception of any individual thing, and Shankara says that fact must have been 'experienced'. The absence of sense-perceptions, and of dream-objects, is known. On waking a man says, 'I did not dream.' (It is true that his memory may be at fault, but this can be applied to testimony about waking also, and does not invalidate the fact that he can make true statements about the past.) He may also say, 'I was happy.' The Indian psychology investigates this statement in great detail. It is not merely that the one going to sleep looks forward to cessation of anxiety; a man who has no anxiety still shows by his behaviour that he looks forward to sleep. In this commentary Shankara adds one more indication, namely that somehow a man asleep is aware of the passing of time. He instances a man in an inner room, shielded from all possible outside clues (like songs of birds, changes of light and so on), who nevertheless knows immediately on waking, 'I have slept a long time' or 'I have slept a short time'. Another commentator cites the cases of men who meditate before sleeping that they want to get up at a particular time, and who do awake at that time. That there are some people who can reliably do this, waking at particular times arbitrarily chosen by others, has been confirmed under laboratory conditions.

A central point is that many people suppose that the statements 'I knew nothing' and 'I did not know' are the same. However, parallel statements about sense-perception show that there is a difference. A blind man in a dark room *does not see*; a normal man with his eyes open *sees nothing* – he can make a statement 'there was nothing visible there'. The blind man cannot make this statement.

Some snakes have organs sensitive to small changes in temperature; they can focus these to detect the location of even a very weak source of heat, for instance a mouse. If this snake is in a dark empty room, it 'heat-senses' nothing, and knows there is no mouse there; a man in that room does not heat-sense, and does not know whether there is a mouse there or not.

To do this meditation the yogi consciously enters into deep sleep. Goethe was evidently aware of one form of it; he wrote in a letter to Humboldt that he had discovered a method of 'entering unconsciousness consciously', and he remarked that it is a secret of inspiration. There are many cases of scientists and artists who found inspiration in their minds on waking from sleep – Helmholtz and Hugo Wolf are examples. Shankara, commenting on a phrase of an Upanishad, says that in deep sleep the individual self is connected with the cosmic energy and is therefore potentially omniscient.

19. The Chosen Form

Sutra 1.39 or (by meditation) on the chosen form

The word for meditation is dhyana, which is the second step of the three stages of meditation. The first was dharana, 'supporting', 'maintaining', where the attention has to be repeatedly brought back to the location of the meditation. In the second step, which comes about after repeated practice of the first, there is a flow of related thoughts and feelings towards the same object, like a stream of oil being poured from one pot to another.

The word for 'chosen' means literally something which specially appeals. It is not unheard of for a teacher to use unexpected things as subjects for meditation in order to teach a particular thing. A man who was an expert in the game called Mah-jong used to visit a Zen teacher once a week, and complained that he could not stay awake in his meditation. 'At first the unfamiliar posture kept me awake, but now it has become very comfortable, and just sitting there with nothing happening – one falls asleep. It's natural, isn't it?'

One day the teacher said to him, 'There is a young pupil who may come here later on. He is the son of a man who likes Mah-jong, and he is forced sometimes to play in his father's circle. But he only knows the bare elements, and they get impatient with him. He does not want to spend much time getting better at it by playing, so I want you to think of some bits of advice by which he can play reasonably and lose not too much. I have to go to see the gardener for about an hour, but meantime would you sit here and think what to say to him if he comes.'

When the teacher returned, his pupil said earnestly, 'I've worked out ten rules for him to follow, and if he sticks to them I can promise that he won't do too badly. You know, there are certain things to look out for, and if you just keep your eye on them, you don't go far wrong. But it needs a lot of experience before you get to know what they are. It hasn't been so easy to express them clearly for a beginner, but I think I can do it now.'

'Thank you very much,' said the teacher. 'You've been here an hour with nothing happening. No trouble with falling asleep?'

The pupil was struck dumb. Then he bowed, and went home.

But for the regular yoga training, Shankara says that the chosen object of meditation must be something which is specially proper from the point of view of steadying the mind for yoga, not something which is specially appealing from other points of view like pleasure and so on. For there is the prohibition to the yogi: 'Even if he should obtain objects, he must never dwell on them in his mind.' The chosen form is therefore a symbol of truth or a form of the Lord, and when he has found one of them which stabilises his mind, he will be able to concentrate steadily on other traditional practices as well.

The element of sceptical cynicism which is innate in the human mind, and which is represented by Mephistopheles in Goethe's *Faust*, always tries to neutralise this kind of practice by suggesting that it is merely creating illusions, illusions possibly beneficial to those believing in them, but still illusions. Yes, it argues, the form of Christ is a symbol, or a radiant calm ocean, but it might as well be anything else. An apple would be as good to the one who accepted it.

Shankara states clearly that the traditional forms given for meditation correspond to actual existence. The scriptural instruction about the Lord's possessing certain qualities, which instruction is given for the purpose of meditation, at the same time proves the existence of a Lord possessing those qualities. And he quotes the yoga sutras to the effect that this may be confirmed face to face: 'from the yogic practices there comes vision of the divine form meditated upon', and this form helps him. The classical forms of the incarnations still exist in a subtle radiant form, and are accessible by meditation; these things, he emphasises, are facts which cannot be set aside.

The forms of the Lord are as real, and in a certain sense more real, than the tables and chairs of ordinary experience or the ultimate particles of the physicist; but they are all part of the projection by the divine actor. The forms are not to be fanatically taken as exclusive of each other; they give different patterns for life. Buddha and Christ showed a pattern of renunciation, without any permanent home; Rama was a king and warrior in lay life; Krishna showed many roles, including musician and dancer, which the Buddha-form and others did not display. The yogi does not in the end 'choose' the form arbitrarily; it would perhaps be truer to say that it chooses him.

In the *Heart of the Eastern Mystical Teaching*, a monk named Gopaldas tells the pupils that the purpose of man's life is to worship the creator; all else is emptiness. The form of the incarnation as the Absolute is not within the grasp of mind or imagination, but the visible form can be meditated upon even by a child. 'If you have faith and try to lead a pure sattvic life, you will be blessed with a vision of the incarnation, at first subjective and later on externalised.' Elsewhere in the book it is explained that devotion to an incarnation is for most people essential to satisfy the emotions.

The great form of the Lord as Time, seen by a disciple in the eleventh chapter of the Gita, was too great to be comprehended by a physical eye, but it was not a subjective hallucination; Shankara points out that it was seen by another man also, who had developed the same 'divine eye', and the modern yogi Rama Tirtha refers to the same fact. Madhusudana in his Gita commentary says that the divine eye is manifested in the samadhi of a yogi.

20. Samadhi

Sutra 1.40 Mastery is when the mind can be steadied on anything from the ultimate in smallness to the ultimate in greatness

The Upanishadic verses quoted in the Chapter of the Self describe Brahman:

> Subtle, finer than a lotus-fibre, he stands covering all;
> Greater than the earth, firm, he stands supporting all.

These are the two extremes, and the Lord is ultimately found in each of them. All the other exercises in training the mind refer to objects between these limits. Shankara sums up by saying that he has mastered the practice who is not interrupted by any opposing thought in his experience of the very small or the very great, or what lies between them. He also adds an interesting comment that all the practices are really the same; it is a question of mastering one and then the others also are accessible easily. These are all exercises to purify and stabilise the mind, and they use the things of the world. Even the divine forms are of the world, though in them the divine actor shows himself more clearly than in other things.

The first step is dharana, persistently holding the attention on to a point like the heart-centre; this develops into dhyana where there is a steady flow of thoughts and feelings all of one kind into the object of meditation; in samadhi, the separate ideas of meditation, meditator, and object of meditation disappear. Only the object remains, filling the whole field of awareness. This cannot happen till the mind has been cleared, at least for the time, of other thoughts.

Samadhi is when the natural restlessness (sarvarthata – 'going to all objects') of the mind has been attenuated and its other capacity one-pointedness (ekagrata) has been brought out, and the mind becomes like a pure crystal, through which the object of meditation appears clearly. Unless the crystal is quite clean and held steady, the object on which it is focused does not shine clearly in it. Dr Shastri often used the modern example of the telescope, whose lenses must be clean and steadily focused.

In the ordinary process of knowing, the object known is mixed up with its name and the concept of it. It is assimilated to them; for example, because we think that the lines of a Doric temple like the Parthenon must be straight, we see them as such, though in fact they are not.

It is well known how the eye scales down the size of things in the foreground; amateur photographers take a picture of a friend in a deck chair which looks a satisfactory picture, but when it comes out they find it seems to be all feet. A man who has volunteered for an experiment in endurance of pain is willing to have a burn inflicted on his arm while he is blindfolded. He endures it, and in some cases, burn blisters result. In fact, he has been touched on the arm by a piece of ice. This experiment has been repeated in laboratories on many occasions, one of them in the department of anatomy at Heidelberg University. There exists a critical review in the literature, though there is apparently no altogether satisfactory account of the fact that the sympathetic action is confined to a defined locality. But it is an example of experience of an event being assimilated to a concept.

In samadhi the confusion with concept and name begins to be dissolved, and at a deeper level the associations with time and space also. This requires a forgetting of all associations, and is technically called 'purification of the memory'. Shankara makes the important point that these things can only really be forgotten when they are recognised to have been illusory. The concepts and names and associations have been super-imposed on the object, as the world of the play is super-imposed on the actor. When they have been forgotten, the object is known as it is, an individual thing free from the super-imposition of universals (concepts like 'hot iron' in the case of the blister experiment). This is the true perception; all ordinary perceptions are mixed up with associations. It is called prajna or insight.

Here is a translation of the commentary of Shankara on the point:

The memory is to be purified from the conventional uses of words, for instance the general consensus, '*This* is the expression for *this*, and *this* is to be expressed by *this*'. The memory produced by the conventional use is the memory of word-association. Washing away of this memory means its cessation by reason of the fact of its illusoriness (being recognised). The purification arises when rajas (passion) and tamas (inertia) have been overcome.

The memory is purified from ideas received from others, even from the scriptures, and from ideas derived from inference, which means from indications. These two, inference and authority, have for their field universals alone. The ideas received from them are a superimposition (adhyaropa) on the particular object. When there is absence of that superimposition (adhyasa) for the yogi in his samadhi-insight, when in other words it is freed from superimpositions of inferential or verbal knowledge, then the samadhi grasps the object in its own nature, as it is, freed from associations of direction, space, time and so on. It is magnified, in its own qualities alone, and does not show anything – space, time or anything else – apart from its own bare nature.

The prajna-insight of the yogi is determined by the bare nature of that object. The prajna does not appear as the ordinary process-of-knowing, for it has no impediment (to be overcome), and it is distinct as the form of the object alone. All the relations superimposed formerly on it have gone. This is the higher perception. The lower perception is common to everyone, and it is mediated by a modification of the mind; but higher perception is had by a yogi alone.

This quotation from Shankara shows that he sees all relations and predicates of an object as ultimately illusory, super-imposed on it. This does not mean that they are valueless, but only that they are not absolutely true. (He uses the technical words adhyasa and adhyaropa for 'illusory super-imposition', which are frequently used in his other commentaries; this is a pointer to the authenticity of the present one.) However even these objects as known in samadhi are themselves only relatively real; though as Shankara says a horse is a real thing, known from daily dealings in the world, it is real only on that level. There are deeper levels – for instance the level of atomic structure, as he points out. And deeper is the mental level of the cosmic mind. The deepest level of the world is bare energy, which appears as the projection by the Lord of the play of the world. The purpose of meditation is not to determine relative realities, but to penetrate through:

> Subtle, finer than a lotus-fibre, he stands covering all;
> Greater than the earth, firm, he stands supporting all.
> He is other than the sense-knowledge of this world.

The world is not different from him, who is ever standing
as the supreme, who is to be known, who himself divides
into many.
From him the bodies all come forth, he is the root,
eternal, he is constant.

In discussing samadhi, it has to be recognised that descriptions of yogic states, not part of ordinary experience, will be increasingly unsatisfactory when judged by ordinary experience and its standards. A man who has never seen the sea will find descriptions of it increasingly incredible; he who has only seen ripples on a little lake will not be able to accept stories about waves eighty feet high round Cape Horn.

To get a hint of samadhi, a student is recommended to create particular circumstances favourable to it. He should get up early and be sitting comfortably on a hill looking towards the east, half an hour before dawn on a clear morning, to watch the sun rising. It is essential that he should not see anything close to him in the line of sight; that sets up reactions in his body. He may be unconscious of them but they can prevent the experience. His vision should go out to the far distance; if he cannot find a hill, he can look out over the sea on a calm day. He watches the lightening of the sky before the dawn, then the edge of the sun coming up, then the whole orb. It is often found on these occasions that there is a partial loss of body consciousness, and absence of the verbal associations 'sun', 'sea' and so on. Many people feel also some great significance which they cannot properly grasp; when they try to verbalise it, there is nothing to lay hold of. But it can give some idea that ordinary experience is partly a mental construct, and this is a help in practising yoga.

Shankara says that such things are samadhi states, but they are not part of yogic training because they are so brief, and obscured by rajas and tamas. In yogic samadhi, the mind has been partially purified; the first stage of it is the same as ordinary perception except that the attention is steady, which in ordinary perception it is not. When samadhi progresses, the associations begin to drop away, internally and externally. When the memory is finally 'purified' and all associations recognised as illusory superimpositions – forgotten, the object, on the level of meditation, becomes radiant. It becomes 'magnified' in the sense that there is nothing else; it fills the whole universe.

When this higher samadhi is repeated again and again on the same object, the yogi becomes 'skilled' in it; it becomes natural to him and it is serene and clear. Then it is 'truth-bearing' – it reveals truth by inspiration. In connection with objects or situations in the world this is like a 'revelation', but inasmuch as it is truth about limited objects, it is still concerned with illusion. This is the purest and most beautiful part of illusion – it corresponds to enjoying the play, and taking part in it, in inner tranquillity, appreciating its beauty and vigorously performing the role which is now clear.

In the Chapter of the Self, the samadhis are of three kinds:

Preliminary – on the highest mental functions like independence, sharing with others, truthfulness. These are the yogas of verse 14.

On Brahman as 'projecting' the whole universe and entering it as consciousness.

On Brahman as the Lord of the 'city', 'hidden in the cave'.

Preliminary are the samadhis on the highest part of the illusion; the others are meditations on truth.

Increasing 'skill' in samadhi comes about because samadhi, like every other experience, produces a dynamic impression in the seed-bed at the root of the mind. The impressions, called sanskaras, are of course of many kinds. They manifest in accordance with a law of association, both positive and negative. At the beginning meditation is constantly interrupted by the emergence into mental awareness of sanskaras which are irrelevant or hostile to the subject of meditation. Each effort at disregarding them and returning to the meditation creates a new sanskara of its own; finally these new sanskaras show themselves at the time of meditation in strength, as a continuous flow of related thoughts and feelings, and the meditation becomes continuous. Sanskaras of meditation on the one object form a mutually reinforcing group, which facilitate meditation on it, and that in turn creates new ones.

Shankara in his Gita commentary remarks that the onrush of passion cannot always be restrained by will alone; only when samadhi has been attained can it invariably be controlled. The Gita says that when assailed by passion, the yogi should sit in a solitary place and practise samadhi. When he has done this for some months, the sanskaras of that samadhi will rise spontaneously at the time of the onrush of anger or other doshas.

Shankara in the Chapter of the Self points out, however, that though the passion may be temporarily pacified, it will return, because the root cause, Ignorance, has not been pulled up. He makes this point repeatedly in his great commentaries. In this commentary, he sets it out at length, explaining how the yogas can overcome the doshas just because yogas are associated with truth and doshas with illusion. The man who has accurate knowledge will defeat, in worldly strife, one who is deluded as to the facts.

The objector is not silenced. He makes the apparently strong point (which at some time or other comes up in the mind of every yogi) that after all yogas and doshas are like opposing armies, and it cannot be assumed that yogas will necessarily defeat the other side. Shankara explains that the yogas only do defeat the doshas when they are associated with knowledge, that is, when the yoga is in fact reinforcing meditation on the Lord and on the Self as the reality, and the world as not absolutely real. Without this knowledge of truth, the yogas do not necessarily defeat the doshas. He says here, and elsewhere also, that in the end the doshas are dissolved by knowledge of truth; the yogas are really a sort of systematic practice of the expressions of knowledge of truth in this world. The negative yogas like freedom from anger are deliberate practice, in meditation and action, of the independence and serenity of the Self; the positive ones like sharing out are systematic practice of realisation of the Lord as standing in all beings equally, the Lord who is to be known, who himself divides into many.

The doshas do not absolutely cease, but they are so thinned out that the reality shines through the transparent veil. There is still movement of the mind, but it is not something which builds up into a persistent attitude of passion. Socrates very rarely showed anger, but when he did, the effect was devastating, as we know from accounts of him in battle, and on a few other occasions. But there was no hate or malice in him; he never showed anger for personal reasons. He met assaults on himself with humour; when his pupils protested that he should prosecute he answered, 'If a donkey kicks me, do you want me to take him to law?'

The objector still persists that even though the doshas may be met and dissipated when they arise, they will go on rising in full force while life lasts, because the sanskaras which cause them remain. The sutra of Patanjali on this is I.50:

> the sanskara produced by the higher samadhi is
> the master of other sanskaras

Shankara comments that the higher samadhi, when it is 'skilful', is truth-bearing, and it de-energises the opposing sanskaras of ordinary experience, which are tainted with illusion. So though the onrush of passion is met when it arises in the mind, it may occur again until the sanskaras which give rise to it have been dissipated by the sanskara produced by repeated higher samadhi. It is true that a slight veil of sanskaras does remain while life lasts, but this is so thin that the truth of the Lord shines through it, and the actions prompted by these very refined sanskaras are for the good of the whole world.

A samadhi on an ordinary object of the world, when it has become 'truth-bearing' dissolves the illusions of time and space and cause-and-effect. But the 'truth' of an ordinary object is only a relative truth, and to integrate the knowledge of it into other experience, some of the illusory super-impositions have to be put back on to it. Still, they are put back in the knowledge that they are illusory, stage props in the cosmic play.

When the samadhi is made on final truth, of the Lord as all-pervading, and as the Self, the sanskaras of it dissolve all the other sanskaras, as the dawn dissolves the illusion of the night whereby a post appears as a man. The post is still seen, but it is no longer mistaken for a man.

As the samadhi becomes 'skilful', its dynamic seeds go into the seed-bed, and the doshas are attacked at their root, Ignorance. For this reason Shankara emphasises that fundamentally it is practice of truth itself which dissolves the doshas; they are not dissolved permanently by samadhi practice alone, because its effect is temporary. The individual yogas of verse 14 are combined with truth – in fact they have to be based on vision of truth, or at least faith in truth. The essence of the process is a change in the seed-bed at the roots of the mind; a violent change of attitude by conscious application of will, or emotional excitement, or intellectual application, does not last unless the seed-bed has been changed. It is not directly accessible to the ordinary functioning of the mind; it consists of sanskaras, dynamic latent impressions, and it is changed by dynamic impressions laid down as a result of continued practice. Until this has been done, sudden conversion in a state of excitement is often followed by a violent reaction. As an indication, it has been said that it takes six weeks of keen application to yoga to make a significant change, three months before the change is apparent to the man himself. In three years there can be a complete and lasting change of the whole roots of the personality.

Thus each stage is first practised deliberately and systematically; as it becomes more and more powerfully represented in the seed-bed, it becomes natural and spontaneous. In the Gita commentary Shankara gives samadhi the highest place in karma yoga, but it has to spread out from the time of meditation to form a background to the whole life. Let a man have a vision of the Lord all the time, he explains, but in so far as he fails to do this, let him practise samadhi on the Lord at fixed times; in so far as he does not attain samadhi even at these favourable times, let him do all his actions for the sake of the Lord, without performing any for his own personal needs; if he cannot do this for all his actions, then he may also perform actions for personal motives, but he must give up attachment to the fruits of them; whether they succeed or fail, he must be independent and self-controlled.

These are the four stages. Shankara remarks that it is not a question of ruling out the higher stages because one is not yet 'ready'. They have to be attempted every day. The continuous vision of the Lord has to be attempted each day, and if it is not continuous (as it cannot be at the beginning) then it must be revived at fixed times of meditation, and if samadhi is not attained, by which all his actions will naturally be for the Lord, then he has to imitate that effect by deliberately making them, doing them in dedication; and in so far as he cannot do this with all of them, let him do some personal actions but holding himself independent and self-controlled. Each lower stage is a purposeful and conscious imitation of the effect which will naturally come about in the higher stage. This is a general principle of yoga training, and of other trainings too – a student of a foreign language learns carefully rules of grammar which later will be used naturally without thinking about them.

Each stage is practised by an effort of will, supported by emotional concentration in the form of devotion, and intellectual concentration in the form of rational conviction. As the stage becomes natural, it springs spontaneously from the sanskaras, and is experienced as will-less joy. There is no will in the consciousness of truth; the will is concerned with removing the obstacles to it.

So for a man at the beginning there is a fourfold exercise of the will, which gradually comes down to a single exercise of it, and then a flooding of the instruments by the divine will, with no individual concerns at all. In the end, no individual will is left.

First stage (1) He must try every day to keep up awareness of the Lord in the universal form, as described for example in the eleventh chapter of the Gita, or the verses of the Chapter of the Self:

> It is great, a mass of splendour, all-pervading, the Lord.
> He who is in all the beings, wise, immortal, firm, without limbs, without sound, without body, without touch, great, pure –
> He is all, the highest goal, he is in the centre, he divides, he is the city.

This awareness, or faith, will frequently lapse.

(2) At fixed times he sits in samadhi practice on it.

(3) Until he attains samadhi experience, he must also deliberately set himself to direct all his actions to cosmic purposes, which he knows of at second-hand from traditions like 'love the neighbour as the Self'. This practice purifies and calms the mind and brings samadhi experience closer in his set meditation periods.

(4) At the beginning he finds he cannot give up all his personally motivated actions, so he must make *some* of his actions for the good of others as an offering to the Lord. He will know whether he has done this by his reactions when they are met with ingratitude, or when they fail completely, or are misused. He may keep his struggle for personal status and comforts and personal attachments, but when he acts for these, he must practise independence and worship. He must not be upset when success produces resentment, when failure produces contempt or accusations. He has

to try to control the rush of thoughts and feelings, to be able to forget both success and failure, pleasure and pain, gain and loss, not anticipating them eagerly or fearfully before they come, nor looking back after they go.

Second stage When he has gained some independence, he is no longer dominated by the pulls of personal wishes, like a marionette on strings.

He now needs to practise only the three steps. *All* his actions he tries to make meaningful in the spiritual sense, and he is able to shake himself free from reacting to their immediate success or failure. The lowest stage is now natural to him. He practises samadhi at the fixed times, and also tries to protect what experience he has by returning to it and reviving it during the day.

Third stage The actions are now naturally for the good of all, and he no longer has to think about them. His practice is samadhi at fixed times, and trying to preserve it during the day.

Fourth stage When samadhi experience comes at the fixed times, he seeks to keep 'yukta' or steady in samadhi, even when perceiving and acting in the world. The consciousness of Self, which at first comes in flashes longer or shorter, he seeks to make continuous. Finally there is a conflagration, where as the Gita says the Lord reveals himself as the Self. Shankara calls this the rise of Knowledge.

Part Three

Knowledge

3. Padmāsana – the Lotus seat, demonstrated by a brahmachārī at Śṛingeri monastery.

4. Siddhāsana – the Perfect seat.

21. Knowledge

In his Gita commentary and elsewhere, Shankara declares repeatedly that meditation is the immediate precursor of Knowledge. Verse 8 in the Chapter of the Self runs:

> The yogi who practises realisation of that in everything,
> and always holds to firmness in that,
> Will see that which is hard to see and subtle,
> and rejoice in heaven.

In the commentary, Shankara defines Ignorance as taking the Self to be limited by such things as mind and body, and Knowledge as knowing the Self as universal, 'a binding of the Knower to Brahman'. He sees it through 'great skill' in samadhi, and the word for skill means the same as the word which occurs in the Patanjali Yoga Sutra on samadhi, 'when there is skill in the higher (samadhi), there comes undisturbed inner calm'.

In the commentary on the next verse, Shankara says that the man of Knowledge sees this first in meditation, with his senses withdrawn; but the man of Brahman even at the time of dealing with the world sees the Self who has entered into all beings. Now the senses and mind are functioning in response to events in the world, but the Self is not felt to be identified with a body and mind. It is universal, 'Brahman, in the highest heaven'.

Self-awareness is universality. 'He becomes all-pervading' are the last words of the Chapter of the Self. There is no individuality in the body and mind of the yogi who has reached liberation. They are like fingers of the Lord and do not act for themselves.

It is often objected that avatars and sages do behave like individuals, some of them with very marked personalities. There is a consistency in their lives and actions; Christ hid from the crowd who wished to make him king, whereas Rama played out his life as a prince and a king. Shankara was a monk and Mohammad a householder. The Jain teachers were lifelong vegetarians, but Peter was a fisherman. Buddha began as a prince and ended as a wandering beggar, whereas Paul insisted on supporting himself by his own trade. If these are all the universal Lord, how is it that the individual characteristics persist?

One answer is that they are different roles, played by an actor who keeps his fundamental identity hidden beneath them, and creates beauty by displaying the appropriate characteristics of the role. It would not be proper for the actor playing Othello to display the same detachment and wisdom as when he plays Prospero. If we say, Could he do it? the answer is that as the actor, he could do it, but as Othello, he could not.

In discussing the world illusion, Shankara sometimes uses examples like the rope which is mistaken for a snake, causing terror in the beholder. The fright disappears when the nature of the rope is known. This example is meant to give an illustration of only the one point, namely super-imposition of a false snake on a real rope. It is not meant to be taken that the world process is an unfortunate chance error. He says again and again when setting forth the Upanishadic accounts of projection that the one important point is that this projection is conscious and purposive, from a supreme divine intelligence. It can best be compared to the illusions projected by a magician for the entertainment of the beholders, or the illusion of the play projected in a drama. The characters of Hamlet and Horatio are indeed 'set up by Ignorance' in the sense that they are not absolutely real; but they are not meaningless. The 'Ignorance' corresponds to the voluntary suspension of disbelief which the audience practises at the beginning of a play. This suspension of disbelief is meant to go far enough to move them very deeply, but not so far as to produce a lasting impression of absolute reality.

The illustration of the actor works best when he is taken as the Eastern story-teller – one man who takes all the parts, and somehow produces an impression of a number of people in lively conversation and vigorous action. He has a minimum of stage props – perhaps only a fan, as in Japan, which becomes a sword, a cup, a staff, a pen and so on. The change of voice and behaviour creates a sort of world whose characters are very distinct; the effect has to be seen to be fully believed.

Another illustration which Shankara gives is that of the dream. Here the one mind stretches out a universe full of people; there is the same reason to believe that these people are conscious selves as there is in the waking state. Supposing that each of them represents a facet of the sleeper's mind, individualised and self-conscious, then the 'fact' of Knowledge will be that this is all one; this fact will seem to contradict the direct experience of multiplicity. It is possible for one dreaming to attain insight that it is all a dream; then the circumstances cease to oppress him.

All these are no more than intellectual ideas, and their purpose is only to pacify the vehement objection, 'But this is impossible', in order to give the mind the chance to settle down in meditation to get a glimpse of what lies behind the thoughts and feelings of multiplicity.

Knowledge is not an intellectual guess or inference or hypothesis. It is a direct experience. But at the beginning this experience is mixed up with the habitual convictions of duality, so it is something extra-ordinary, and cannot be integrated into ordinary life.

One sees him as a wonder; and so also another speaks of him as a wonder; and as a wonder another hears of him; and though hearing, none understands him at all. (Gita II.29)

Shankara comments on this that one sees the Self as a wonder, as something never seen before, as something strange, seen suddenly. And though seeing him, though hearing and speaking of him, they do not understand him.

They do not understand what it is, because the direct knowledge is confused with super-impositions of Ignorance. When the disciple sees the great vision of the Lord, in the eleventh chapter of the Gita, he does not understand it as the Self at all. He is terrified, and asks that it be withdrawn. He feels it as something infinitely great and strange, and nothing to do with his Self, which he still believes to be his own body, mind, and role in life. This shows clearly in what he says at the time. In the vision of the universal, he sees all the worlds and their inhabitants, and he is also shown a glimpse of the future, to help him perform his own proper role in the light of the memory of it. In that glimpse he sees some of the figures with which his present role is concerned, and among them that of his great opponent Karna. The disciple Arjuna is of royal birth, and Karna is believed to be the son of a charioteer. Even at this moment of vision, Arjuna exclaims, 'I see the hosts of warriors, Bhishma, Drona and that son of a charioteer ...' He was firmly locked into his own individual role, with its attendant prejudices, and could not see the Self in all. So the vision passed, and though he had exaltation through it, he did not attain Knowledge.

What is beyond super-impositions can only be thought about by re-imposing some of them again, and the Brahman beyond all super-impositions is thought of in terms of attributes like the projection of the universe, and the individualities imagined in it, and the presiding Lord who is the friend of all. The human mind without experience tends to think that Brahman must be either without attributes, or with attributes – it cannot be both. When he has experience, he can accept that Brahman is both without attributes and with them, as the English actor playing Brutus both is and is not a Roman and playing Cerimon both is and is not a doctor.

In his Brahma-sutra commentary, Shankara sums up the point: the creation comes from the supreme Brahman through its unlimited powers. The Upanishads say that the Lord is omniscient and omnipotent. If it be objected that the Upanishads also say that the supreme Brahman has no attributes, being described as 'Not this, not this', the answer is that reasoning cannot apply to the supreme Brahman which is to be known from the Upanishads alone. Although all attributes are indeed denied, still Brahman has all powers of creation and so on which Brahman projects as illusion. So the Upanishad says, 'He moves and grasps without feet and hands, He sees without eyes, and hears without ears.'

The Gita recommends that the mind should not try to dwell on Brahman without attributes, but rather on Brahman with attributes, which is approachable by the mind.

The technical reason is, that the remaining sanskaras representing the unexhausted karma keep the mind engaged in its remaining role in life, and this role can be understood and carried out in connection with the divine attributes by expressing the divine attributes, especially the attribute of the Lord as friend of all. Brahman without attributes is not expressed by any role in life.

The purpose of creation is an overflowing of joy as a sort of sport, not as a compulsion; the illustration is a man singing a song, creating beauty out of mere joy. Dr Shastri asked his pupils to find the thread of beauty in the world creation, and seek to embody it in some way in thought and activity as well as realise it in meditation. There are a number of descriptions of the rise of Knowledge in the Gita, and of the man in whom Knowledge has risen. Of course these descriptions have to use the super-impositions of words to direct the attention to what is beyond words; it is something like the use of perspective to point the attention to a third dimension, into the canvas itself. Here are a few of the passages:

The enlightened one is he who knows that the Self does no action

The enlightened man has seen the Self

... has acquired a knowledge of the Self

... has a clear Knowledge (viveka-jnana) of Self

... is unshaken by gunas

... his joy is in the Self, he knows the Self

... sees the supreme

... sees the oneness of Self and the Lord

... has realised the true nature of the Self

... has attained right vision (samyag-darshana)

... knows the truth and sees the supreme reality

... realises Brahman as the Self

... knows the real nature of the Lord

... worships the imperishable, devoid of attributes

... sees no distinctions ... sees rightly

... is free from delusion

... perceives in the Self no pain whatever

... awakens to the immutable Self
... distinguishes the Self from what is not Self

The Chapter of the Self refers to the 'pandit'; this can mean a learned man, and has been anglicised as 'pundit'. But Shankara says in his commentary,

Delusion does not disappear simply by a view arising merely out of words. He sees it first in meditation ... Having thrown off the doshas which torment beings, the pandit attains peace. Here pandit is used in the sense of knower of Brahman, not a knower of doctrine.

Knowledge as used by Shankara must not be confused with the knowledge of the world through the senses, for the text says, 'He is other than the sense-knowledge of this world'; nor is it the system of inferences and hypotheses called science; nor is it academic learning of revealed texts. These things do not remove delusion and grief, nor do they give immortality. And the text says, 'Those who realise it, they are immortal.'

Great academic learning is sometimes a refuge from practice, and the compulsion to study the details can become a way of having no time for the main thing. There is a traditional teaching story on the point.

In the middle of the nineteenth century, a famous scholar made every year a lecture tour of towns in northern India, to speak on Vedanta. He used to hire little horse carriages to transport him between towns when there was no railway. Once he had some difficulty in finding a carriage to take him the next stretch of about twenty miles, and he realised he would have to walk. His hosts did not seem able to find even a porter willing to go in that direction, but in the end a man turned up and they set out.

In conversation on the way, the pandit discovered that the porter knew his name and that he lectured each year. The porter said, 'I couldn't afford to go to the lecture, and anyway I wouldn't have understood it, but I heard about the title of the one which you gave in our town last year. It was "The Lord standing equally in all beings". I often thought about it.'

'Well, the lecture would have been perhaps rather difficult for you,' remarked the scholar. 'But I think I showed that the concept appears already in the Skambha of the Atharva, for instance; my title I took of course from the dialogue in the sixth book of Mahabharata, the Gita I expect you would call it.'

'It must be wonderful to be a great scholar,' replied the porter, 'I was so happy to have the honour of carrying your luggage.'

'How was it that everyone was unwilling to come this way?' asked the pandit casually. The porter made an evasive answer, but this roused the other's curiosity, and in the end he admitted, 'The fact is that there is a lion in this area which is a bit lame, so it can't catch its prey. It has a habit of attacking travellers, and we porters don't like going this way. No, sir, it would be no good turning back now; we've already passed most of the dangerous part, and it'll be safer to go on.'

Soon afterwards, a lion appeared round a rock. The porter dropped the luggage and jumped in front of the pandit. 'My Lord,' he said, 'this is a great scholar who is doing so much good to our neighbourhood with his lectures. If you are hungry, please take me as your dinner.'

The lion looked at him and went quietly away.

They went on in silence, and then the pandit whispered, 'What happened there?' The porter was rather reluctant to say anything, but the pandit asked again and again, and then he told him,

'I used to think about the title of your lecture last year. They said it had been marvellous, the educated people did. But I thought it must be nonsense – how can the Lord be standing equally in all beings? And then I thought, well, he's a famous scholar, and if he says so it must be true. It used to come to my mind when I was on the journeys. I was looking at the birds and trees and men, and wondering where is the Lord in them? One day I saw something, just for a moment, and since then the thought has never left me. When that lion came out, I saw the Lord looking at me out of his eyes. And I thought, perhaps today the Lord will take me to himself. That's all.'

'Why,' said the scholar, 'I have spent my life and made my name studying the items on the menu, but inwardly I have been starving. You read only one line of it, but you ate the food.'

22. Knowledge-yoga

In the Chapter of the Self, there is first an instruction to perform yoga to purify and steady the mind. Then come the verses on the Self, indicating it from two directions: the king of the city, hidden among his ministers in the innermost apartment, and the creator, sustainer and withdrawer of the universe. It is said that the Self is first known in meditation (verse 9). This is now realisation of everything in the Self and the Self in everything, and he who is seeing thus is Brahman, glorious in the highest heaven and in everything.

And yet in verse 11, as explained by Shankara, it is only when the doshas have been thrown off that this pandit who knows the Self is fully liberated.

The point comes up again and again in his commentaries, in various forms. In many places in the Gita commentary it is said that the rise of Knowledge 'qualifies' for jnana-yoga, or Knowledge-yoga, which leads to liberation. It is described in a number of passages, of which certain verses of chapter XVIII are typical:

> The yogi with pure buddhi, firmly self-controlled, gives up the objects of sense and puts away desire and hate;
>
> Lives in a solitary place, eating little; holding under control speech body and mind, he practises meditation and samadhi, keeping away passion;
>
> Freed from egoism, force, pride, desire, anger and possession, unselfish, serene – he is ready to become Brahman.

This Gita passage refers to a man who has performed the duty and actions to which he was fitted innately, as karma-yoga. That is to say, without attachment to the distant 'fruits' of his actions, as an offering to the Lord, practising indifference to the events of life, and practising devotion-meditation. (It is important to note again that in this doctrine, a man who simply does his duty well, but turns his back on the worship of a supreme which must be stirring in him, does not attain Knowledge.) He has done this, and Knowledge has risen in him. Now the man of Knowledge, with his mind in samadhi, strives to reach the Lord, firm in the faith that he himself is the Lord (Shankara on Gita VII, 18). How can he strive to reach the Lord if he already knows that he himself is that Lord?

In his usual way, Shankara clarifies the point by putting objections into the mouth of an opponent, and meeting them by rational argument. He does not attempt to prove the text by rational argument, but he uses it to meet objections, for instance accusations of inconsistency in the texts.

The main objection which comes up here is that it is inconsistent for the texts to give instructions to perform yoga to a man of Knowledge. Here there is a Self-knower, who by definition is one with the universal Brahman, and yet he has to perform yogas in order to attain Brahman. It would follow that Knowledge does not give liberation. The contradiction is clear-cut: either the Knowledge gives liberation, in which case the instruction to practise yoga along with Knowledge is pointless, or Knowledge does not give liberation, in which case the whole doctrine falls to the ground; either the Knowledge gives universality, in which case there is no one to whom instruction could apply, or it does not, in which case the claim that Knowledge gives universality is wrong.

The answer in the commentary is that knowledge of Self may in some cases not be absolutely clear; in other words the Knowledge may be for a time clouded, not indeed with illusions, but with *memories* of illusions. This is not in every case, but in some cases the memories caused by activities before the rise of Knowledge go on reverberating, even after the rise of Knowledge.

We are familiar in modern life with many cases where mutually inconsistent ideas are held at the same time. In the television serials, when a favourite character complains of a headache or a cold, letters recommending favourite remedies are received at the station, addressed to the character. Such letters are received in tens and occasionally in hundreds. The writers are in a sense aware that the headache or cold is only part of the script, but on the other hand they have actually seen and heard the character complaining, and the illusory idea somehow becomes real enough to make them perform their act of kindness. The confusion may be greater or less; in some cases the letters are addressed to the actor or actress, showing that the two levels of reality are present together at the same time in the mind of the writers, though they would be mutually exclusive if analysed.

In some primitive countries, when the cinema was first introduced, the exhibitors had to be careful not to show an actor or actress dying in one film, and then alive in a film following within the next month or so. There were disturbances among the audiences when the second film was announced, 'No, no, she is dead; we saw her die.'

In all such cases, if the people concerned sit down calmly, not merely to think out but to feel the true state of things, the compelling power of the illusion disappears. This is the natural state of affairs; sitting down calmly is not producing something new, but removing the unnatural disturbances.

In yoga, once Knowledge has arisen there can never again be complete illusion, but sometimes, as Shankara says in his

Brihadaranyaka commentary for example, the memories of previous illusion can make a disturbance and confuse the clearness of Knowledge. It is for these cases that the 'instructions' to perform yoga are given. They are instructions only in form. Before Knowledge, the yogi is an individual, and performs practices, making a time to sit deliberately, deliberately cutting off involvements in thoughts of ordinary life, and concentrating deliberately on the Lord or the Self.

After Knowledge, there is no injunction to do these things. To sit is the natural position for a man who is not being pulled by something; to be at peace is natural for a man who is not entangled in the world; to be aware of universality is natural when there is no illusory imprisonment in individuality. Shankara adds, 'There is no need of an injunction to meditate on the Self, because it is natural to do so.'

What then is the meaning of the directions, 'Practise yoga', 'the wise man should restrain the senses, withdrawing them as a tortoise withdraws his limbs, and remain in samadhi on the Lord, in the form "I am no other than He".' 'By whatever cause the wavering and unsteady mind wanders away, from that let him restrain it and bring it back direct under the control of the Self?'

The reply is, that these are not directions to do something which is natural, but reminders not to do something unnatural which would interfere with it. As an example, take the case of relatives who are sitting up in turns with a fever patient. When the relief comes, she says, 'I am here now, sleep.' Often the previous watcher somehow does not go and sleep at once, but talks a little out of a sort of politeness. The relief says again, 'Sleep, please sleep.' This is in the form of an injunction, but it does not mean that. Someone who has been up all night *will* sleep, and in any case sleep is not a voluntary action to be commanded. 'Sleep!' means 'Don't keep yourself awake any more, don't talk to me, don't feel you have any more responsibility, don't do anything to interfere with the sleep which you should now enjoy.' The apparent injunction is called technically a 'restrictive injunction' in the Vedanta philosophy – it is a short way of ruling out all other alternatives, so that the natural tendency to sleep has its way.

Again, guests hungry from a long journey sit down and politely wait till the host is served, but he says to them, 'Eat, please eat.' For hungry men to eat food in front of them does not need a command; the word 'eat!' is a restrictive injunction, telling them not to wait out of politeness when the host is wanting them to satisfy their hunger straight away.

After Knowledge, the karma-already-in-operation, namely the undertakings and obligations and promises and so on which a man has assumed in his present role in life, still produces likes and dislikes, though the objects are known to be illusory. The injunctions to meditate are to prevent these memories from reinforcing each other. When left alone they die out.

For instance, to Knowledge, the functioning of the world is a conscious movement, purposeful and beautiful. But memories of the materialist view may bring up the conviction that it is like an unconscious mechanism. 'If a ball is struck, it flies off; the movement can be predicted and calculated. Its flight is the resultant of blind forces – there is no need to suppose any conscious controller.' The Knower throws off that view of unconscious cause-and-effect sequence. The predictions can indeed be made, but they are the same thing as predicting the next note of a tune that one knows. Each note is a conscious free expression of the universal Musician; the earlier notes do not cause the later ones, though there is a relation between them which may be partly known.

It may be said: 'What is the difference in practice between a mechanical cause-and-effect sequence and the notion of free expression on pre-determined lines?' It is the difference between a pianola and a master pianist. With the former, the notes are all played, in their sequence, but there is little beauty; they are all at the same strength. With the musician, there are shades of intonation which give expression to the music. The musician has himself chosen the music freely; he does not now express his freedom by altering the notes, though of course he could do so. His freedom is in maintaining the sequence of the notes; contrary to the assumptions of the materialist, unless there were an intelligent controller, the surface order would lapse into chaos. Even the materialist assumptions, if carried to their logical conclusion, must predict ultimate chaos, because it is accepted that at the most fundamental level there is uncertainty. Suppose a simple wheel, mounted without friction so that it can turn freely around its axis, which passes through the centre of the wheel. If the wheel is set in movement by an initial turn, it will keep on moving indefinitely. Since there is always some uncertainty in the initial velocity, if we wait sufficiently long, the position of the wheel will be completely undetermined. This is one of the reasons why Shankara insists that there must be an intelligent controller of even the simplest movements of nature, like water flowing. He says that the control is exercised from within, by the Lord as the inner controller.

The yogis say that they hear the master musician or flute player who plays the whole universe; they see the puppet-master who manipulates the movements of the cosmos, a simile used also by Albert Einstein.

When attention is turned to the Lord as the controller, the memories of the other conviction die away; many things are seen which the superficial vision of the materialist overlooks, or deliberately brushes aside. The so-called causation is not the true causation; we may think we can successfully exploit the regularities and to some extent we can do so. But we find that the regularities conceal deeper and deeper complexities, which cannot be manipulated so easily. The regularities cannot be isolated in closed systems. Science advances by studying repetitions, but there are no exact repetitions, and as we approach the edge of precision we find the regularities dissolving into something else. Materialism cannot explain the evolution of complex forms of life when the simple forms are just as successful in terms of propagation. The yogis do not turn their back on science, but they know that the sequences which science studies are not determined by unconscious 'laws of nature'; there has to be intelligence. After all, why these laws of nature and not others? The regularities are the regularities of a play, and they can be different in different plays. Ariel and Puck can fly; Lear and Brutus cannot. Rama Tirtha sums it up saying that to see cause-and-effect is to fall, and to see the controller Lord is freedom.

While body and mind last, they express Knowledge in action and speech through the memory of cause and effect, in terms which other people can understand. But sometimes those terms are transcended. Swami Rama Tirtha gives an account of a yogi who was chanting Om when he was attacked by an old tiger. A man who witnessed this from a cliff said that the yogi's voice went on chanting the Om without any change as the tiger tore off an arm, and only stopped when the tiger killed him. Rama Tirtha himself, a strong and daring swimmer, was caught in a whirlpool;

he made three attempts to get out, and when he failed, cried, 'If it is to go, then let it go – Om, Om, Om!' He was carried down and drowned. In many lesser ways also, Knowledge shows itself to give faith and courage to the people of the world. In a ship in a typhoon off the China coast, the crew gave up hope and rushed to get drunk at the bar. Dr Shastri, who was a passenger, began to chant in a loud voice the name of Buddha – Namu Amida Butsu. Some of the passengers took it up, and then some of the crew also. Their courage was restored and the boat was saved.

23. Freedom

Analogies, inferences, illustrations, instances – these can never be more than encouragement to faith and practice. They may seem to give certainty, but that is only while circumstances remain favourable. Religious communities without real experience, as Hakuin pointed out, can be like trees with interlacing branches which have died at the root, but which support each other. They seem firm, but when a gale comes everything goes down.

To try to discuss freedom in words and concepts which are products of individuality-experience becomes self-defeating. Human beings inevitably think of a 'liberated man' as somehow like themselves, but with perhaps some 'insight' or 'change of view-point'. The thought that there is no individual man there at all, but the universal Self moving that body and mind, can indeed be verbalised; but then somehow it is supposed that there must be an individual watching the activity going on, like a man aware that his teeth are chattering. There are those who believe that by following out instinctive drives they are somehow part of the 'cosmic will'; they forget that instinctive drives are centred round individual and species, and so based on illusion.

The iron prison keeps its grip until man seeks through yogic practice to find what he really is. Mephistopheles whispers, 'This is a prisoner dreaming that he is free; it may give him a temporary respite, but it is all nothing. It is really infantile – a child in a storm at sea closing its eyes and imagining it is safe home in bed.'

Yoga practice is not a dream. There is one case where closing the eyes to the storm and imagining one is in bed is not infantile, and that is when it corresponds to the facts, when the storm is a dream, dreamed by one in bed. In the years following the French Revolution it was not uncommon for the ruling class in various countries to dream that they were themselves French aristocrats about to be executed. When they were forced down beneath the guillotine, with eyes closed or bandaged, in some cases the thought came, 'If only this were a dream!' Then when the blade came down, they awoke, and it was.

Even in the most terrifying dream there is something which knows it is not completely real. This is shown by the fact that experiences which would leave a terrible wound if met in waking are vividly passed through in dream but forgotten quickly. In the same way, there is something in waking experience which is not completely submerged in it, but has a vague idea of something beyond. It is impossible to live in the conviction that this world is a mental construct unless there have been yogic experiences; but the yogic texts, if attended to, make a stir in the depths below the personality.

A bird which has been kept in a cage, even a large one where it can fly, is uneasy when it is freed. It sits on a branch and watches the wild birds flying past, and hears their songs. Its wings quiver, and it seems to try to fly, but the conviction of imprisonment settles on it and it gives up. It is, observers say, sometimes only after many painful efforts that it finally arrives at the practical conviction that it is free. It can of course see that it is free, but the memory of the bars has bound it.

The yogic texts make a quiver in the seed-bed at the root of the mind; as a famous Zen phrase says, they are a sword thrust into the seed-bed. Yogic practice does not actually accomplish anything new, but it removes the obstacles to the full manifestation of that obscure awareness of freedom which is innate in man, beyond practical everyday life, beyond the defensive cynicism of intellect, beyond the darkness of the seed-bed.

Here are the verses on the Self in the Apastamba Law-book again:

> Each and every living being is the city belonging to the one
> lying at rest in the cave, indestructible, taintless,
> the unmoving abiding in the moving.
> Those who practise realisation of it, they are immortal.
> This indeed which here in this world and here in that world is called the object –
> Having shaken himself free from it, let the seer devote himself to that which lies in the cave.
> He who is constant in all beings, wise, immortal, firm, without limbs, without sound, without body, without touch, great, pure –
> He is all, the highest goal, he is in the centre, he divides, he is the city.
> The yogi who practises realisation of that in everything, and always holds to firmness in that,
> Will see that which is hard to see and subtle, and rejoice in heaven.
> The seer meditating, seeing everything in the Self, will not be deluded,
> And whoever sees the Self alone in everything,
> He is Brahman, glorious in the highest heaven.
> Subtle, finer than a lotus-fibre, he stands covering all;
> Greater than the earth, firm, he stands supporting all.
> He is other than the sense-knowledge of this world.
> The world is not different from him, who is ever

standing as the supreme, who is to be known, who
himself divides into many.
From him the bodies all come forth, he is the root,
eternal, he is constant.

Part Four

Appendices

5. Sukhāsana – the Easy seat.
This is the meditation posture recommended to laymen.

Appendix 1

THE CHAPTER OF THE SELF (HISTORICAL)

The significance of the Chapter of the Self of the Āpastamba Law-book in the history of early Vedānta is discussed in detail in Professor Hajime Nakamura's *Shoki Vedānta Tetsugaku-shi* (History of Early Vedanta Philosophy), the first volume of which covers Vedānta before the Brahma-sūtras. Professor Nakamura has kindly agreed to the inclusion here of a translation of the relevant section as follows (notes giving references are largely omitted).

In India from early times a great number of law-books were composed. They lay down, from a Brahminical standpoint, structures, customs and daily activities of society, concentrating on such problems as the systems of four castes and the four stages of life (āśrama). At first they were written in the comparatively concise sūtra style and their contents also were brief and simple, but later on elaborate law-books containing also civil and criminal law were produced. These were compiled and edited by the priestly Brahmins, and the outlook of Brahminism is clear in them. Among Buddhist texts the Vinaya-Piṭaka, which is one of the Tripiṭaka, should be classed as a kind of law-book, but this is a legal work applicable only to the order of monks and not to society at large, whereas the law-books edited by the Brahmins purport to be rules and regulations for society in general, and are completely different in significance from the Vinaya-Piṭaka. These law-books compiled by the Brahmins have been highly regarded as most valuable sources for information about social conditions in ancient India, though on the other hand some scholars assert that they are simply Utopias composed by Brahmins of the priestly class, remote from actual conditions of society in ancient India. Thorough-going investigation would be needed to clarify the historical and social significance of the Brahminical law-books, but I shall not now enter into the problem. I will content myself with remarking that since these law-books are works by the Brahmins, they are valuable sources for information about their *thought*. It is needless to say that Vedānta thought expounded in them rates highly as revealing one aspect of the history of Vedānta philosophy.

Among the ancient law-books, it is specially in the Āpastamba-dharma-sūtra that Vedānta thought appears. This work has been considered as one section of the Kalpasūtra belonging to the Āpastamba school, a Black Yajurveda school in southern India, and it is one of the oldest extant law-books. In I.8.22 and 23 of this work, Vedāntic ideas are explained, particularly in the section called the Adhyātma-paṭala (Chapter of the Self), on which there exists a commentary ascribed to Śaṅkara which has been published, and which is called the Adhyātma-paṭala-vivaraṇa.

The authenticity of the commentary has been called into question. But in its quotations it restricts itself almost entirely to the ancient Upanishads, and its literary style resembles that of Śaṅkara. Moreover as a commentary it is far more accurate than the Ujjvāla-vṛitti of Haradatta, which is a commentary on the entire Āpastamba-dharma-sūtra, and since it is also apparent that its author was versed in Vedic Sanskrit, it may well be by Śaṅkara. Even if it is not an authentic work by him, I would think that it may be put in the same category – it must, in other words, have been written by a scholar of learning and upbringing similar to Śaṅkara at a period not too far from his. In the Āpastamba-dharma-sūtra, sūtra 22.4–23.3 of the Adhyātma-paṭala section are quotations from authoritative works prior to the law-book. As the commentator Śaṅkara says, they may be citations from some Upanishads composed before that time, but not found in any extant Upanishads. But the following are very much like the Kāṭhaka Upanishad:

Adhyātma-paṭala	*Kāṭhaka Upanishad*
4 ahanyamāna (indestructible, lit. not-struck-down)	II.18 na hanyate hanyamāne śarīre (he is not slain when the body is slain). 19 nayam hanti na hanyate (this slays not nor is slain). (Compare Chāndogya VIII.10.4; na vadhenāsya hanyate (by killing of this, he is not killed); Gītā II.19 and 20: na hanyate hanyamāne śarīre; hanti kam? (whom does he slay?))
4, 5 guhāśaya (lying in the cave)	III.12 eṣa sarveṣu bhuteṣu gūdhātmā (this atman concealed in all beings). III.1 guhām praviṣṭau (who have entered the cave). IV.6, 7 guhām praviśya (having entered the cave). (Cp. Svet. VI.11 eko devaḥ sarvabhūteṣu gūḍhaḥ. (one god hidden in all beings).)

4 te 'mṛtāḥ (bhavanti) (they become immortal).	VI.9 amṛtās te bhavanti (they become immortal) VI.8 amṛtatvam ca gacchati (he goes to immortality). VI.15 amṛto bhavati (he becomes immortal). VI.16 amṛtatvam eti (he goes to immortality).
5 kavi (seer) (= medhāvin Śaṅkara)	III.14 kavi (= medhāvin, Śaṅkara)
6 tejaskāya (mass of splendour)	V.15 tam eva bhāntam anubhāti sarvaṃ tasya bhāsā sarvam idam vibhāti (he shining, all shine; through his light all this is bright). (Compare: Muṇḍaka II.2.10: same as Kāṭhaka V.15 above; and Svet. VI.14, same.) (See also the Upanishadic illustration of sparks from a fire.)
6 sarvatra nihitaṃ. (all-pervading)	I.14 viddhi tvan etan nihitaṃ guhāyām (know you this to be established in the hidden place). V.10 sarvabhūtāntarātman (the self within all beings).
6 mahāntaṃ (great) ... sarvatra nihitaṃ.	II.20, IV.4 mahāntaṃ vibhum (great all-pervading)
7 nityo vipaścid amṛto dhruvaḥ (constant, wise, immortal, firm)	II.18 *na jāyate mriyate vā vipaścin* nayaṃ kutaś cin na babhūva kaścit, ajo *nityaḥ śāśvato* 'yam purāṇo (the wise self is neither born nor dies, it did not originate from anything nor did anything

	originate from it. It is birthless, eternal undecaying and ancient).
7 anango 'śabdo 'śarīro 'sparśaś ca (without limbs, without sound, without body, without touch)	III.15 *aśabdam asparśam* arūpam avyayam tathā 'rasam (without sound, without touch, without form, without decay, without taste).
7 sa sarvam paramā kaṣṭhā (he is all, the highest goal, peak)	III.11 *kaṣṭhā sa para* gatiḥ (he is the culmination, he is the highest goal). VI.10; paramā gatiḥ (the supreme goal).
8 durdarsaṃ nipuṇaṃ	I.21 na hi suvijñeyam aṇur eṣa dharmaḥ (being subtle, this matter is not easy to understand). II.12 *durdarśaṃ* gūḍham anupraviṣṭaṃ inaccessibly, located in the cave). (According to Jacob's Concordance, this word is found only in the Kāṭhaka Upanishad.)
8 modeta viṣṭape (rejoices in heaven)	I.12,18 modate svargaloke (rejoices in heaven).
9 nākapṛṣṭhe virājati (glorious in highest heaven)	III.16 Brahma-loke mahīyate (glorified in the world of Brahman).
āṇīyān bisorṇāyā ... varṣīyāṃś ca pṛthivyāḥ	II.20 anor aṇīyān mahato mahīyān ātmā (subtler than the subtle and greater than the great, the self).

Some of the words, expressions, ideas and so on in the Ādhyatma-paṭala are common also to other Upanishads, but as shown above, those identical or similar to the Kāṭhaka Upanishad are overwhelmingly conspicuous, in nearly every sūtra of the Ādhyatma-paṭala in fact. It is moreover especially to be noted that the Ādhyatma-paṭala, according to its opening and closing sūtras, aims to teach the yoga concerning Ātman (adhyātmika-yoga), and the Kāṭhaka Upanishad (II.12) teaches that one should realise the state of final release by means of the yoga concerning Atman (adhyātma-yoga). According to Jacob's Concordance, this technical term is used only in this passage of the Kāṭhaka Upanishad, of all the Upanishads with which he dealt. From the above facts we must concede a remarkable resemblance between the Ādhyatma-paṭala and the Kāṭhaka Upanishad. This may lead us to the following conclusion.

As already discussed, the Kāṭhaka Upanishad was composed during the period 350–300 B.C. by one or more of the new poet-thinkers who had a different standpoint from that of the ancient Vedic theologians, and in the same stream of thought were composed other Upanishads remarkably like the Kāṭhaka Upanishad. At present these are not extant, but a very limited portion of them has been transmitted, as quotations, in the Ādhyatma-paṭala of the Apastamba-dharma-sutra. Since the composition of these Upanishads may have been around the same time as the Kāṭhaka Upanishad, the date of the Ādhyatma-paṭala would be at the earliest 300–250 B.C. The date of the present form of the Āpastamba-dharma-sūtra can be neither earlier than that, nor very much later.

So far it has generally been accepted on the basis of George Bühler's study that the Āpastamba-dharma-sūtra was composed in the fourth or fifth century B.C. His grounds were as follows: since the style and use of words in the Āpastamba-dharma-sūtra display archaic forms not in accordance with the rules of Pāṇini's grammar, either the author did not know the Pāṇini grammar (about 350 B.C.) or he knew it but did not think it important. The archaic forms of the book are not deliberate, for the irregularities in this text are peculiar to itself alone, and cannot be found elsewhere. The Āpastamba-dharma-sūtra (I.2.5.4 *et seq.*) calls the famous Svetaketu, who appears in the Śatapatha-Brāhmaṇa and the Chāndogya Upanishad, a 'man of latter days' (avara), so it should have been written in a period not too remote from that of this Old Upanishad. Therefore (concluded Bühler) we may say it belongs to the fifth or fourth century B.C. However, these grounds as they stand are weak and flimsy. The fact that the text does not agree with the grammatical rules of Pāṇini does not permit the inference that it was composed prior to Pāṇini. In view of the very nature of sutra works, special usages are to be expected in them. But since it can be taken that by the time of Patañjali (about 150 B.C.), Pāṇini's grammar was relied upon and in general use among scholars, it may be well to judge that this work came into existence prior to that date. Again there is no necessity to suppose that because Svetaketu is called a 'man of latter days', the date of the Āpastamba-dharma-sūtra is close to that of the Chāndogya Upanishad. Pāṇini clearly states that there are two kinds of Brāhmaṇas, those of ancient date and those recent. Kātyāyana (about 250 B.C.) regards as a 'man of latter days' the famous Yājñavalkya who appears in both the Brāhmaṇas and the Upanishads, and calls him his 'contemporary' (tulyakāla). For these reasons it is possible to think that there is a gap of several centuries between the Āpastamba-dharma-sūtra and Svetaketu, even though the sutra calls him a 'man of latter days'. Therefore it is not at all unreasonable to suppose that the Dharma-sutra assumed its present form in 300–250 B.C. (or even later than that). But since there seem to be also a great number of old elements in this work, handed down and written before that time but put together finally only in this period, further investigation is required.

The Ādhyatma-paṭala is systematically arranged. In the first two sutras it gives an outline of religious practice; next it quotes passages from Upanishads which expound Ātman, and it concludes by listing various virtues as a regimen for practice. In Vedic texts, various virtues are taught here and there, but we do not find vices and virtues systematically contrasted with each other as they are here. So that even in his listing of the virtues we can observe a *systematic attitude* on the part of the editor of the law-book.

Again, the Upanishadic passages quoted in the Ādhyatma-paṭala are not strung together casually, but are all of them concerned with clarification of the nature of Ātman. Even the Kāṭhaka Upanishad, which perhaps was composed in the same period as these passages and is also closely connected with them, comprises not only this kind of symbolic explanation of the nature of Ātman but has also various extraneous arguments and not a few somewhat obscure allegorical expressions. This tendency is notable especially in the Ancient Upanishads. But the Ādhyatma-paṭala selects and quotes *only* passages which explain *clearly* and directly what Ātman is. Accordingly we can infer a special attitude or standpoint of the editor from his method of using quotations. He is *selective* in regard to the Upanishadic texts, and this attitude or standpoint can perhaps be said to be Vedāntic. The Āpastamba-dharma-sūtra nowhere refers to any Vedānta school, nor was the editor himself probably conscious of the fact that such a standpoint is Vedāntic. But we can recognise in it the first shoots of the Vedānta.

Since this Ādhyatma-paṭala explains so clearly the nature of Ātman, in later Vedānta it is regarded as important, so much so that it is quoted by both Śaṅkara and Rāmānuja in their commentaries on the Brahma-sūtra, and, as already pointed out, there is even a commentary ascribed to Śaṅkara.

As for the thought of the Ādhyatma-paṭala, it is on major points almost the same as that of the Kāṭhaka Upanishad. Ātman is the essence of all, including not only the human but all varieties of living being. It is the greatest and at the same time the smallest, hidden in the innermost recess in all individual selves. The fact that all living beings, that is to say, individual selves, are called 'city' specially reminds us of Rāmānuja's philosophy, according to which all spiritual beings and the material world constitute the 'body' of the absolute. Ātman as the absolute is also said by the Ādhyatma-paṭala to be good, eternal, constant, great, pure, immortal, wise, stainless, supreme, root, auspicious, lord, and so on. These attributes are used in other Upanishads as well and are not to be regarded as peculiar to the Ādhyatma-paṭala.

As to religious practice, it teaches the yoga of meditating on and worshipping Ātman. It calls the state of final release 'peace' (kṣema). It clearly allows that final release is attained in the present existence. On the other hand, expressions such as 'He ... will rejoice in heaven' and 'The wise man ... shines forth in the highest world of heaven' point to the notion that complete release is attained in heaven after death.

The Upanishadic passages quoted in the Ādhyatma-paṭala are chiefly concerned with the life of the wandering mendicant, but at the end of the chapter it lays down that one ought to practise the yoga of meditation on Ātman throughout all the four stages of life, i.e. student, householder, forest-dweller, and wandering mendicant. Thus in regard to the problem which engaged the attention of later centuries, namely 'Should one who meditates on Ātman become a wandering mendicant or is he permitted to lead the life of a householder?' the author of the Āpastamba-dharma-sūtra does not definitely come down on one side or the other. He must have thought that every member of the Aryan society should practise the virtues listed.

Why, one may ask, did the author of the Āpastamba-dharma-sūtra compose an Ādhyatma-paṭala of this kind? It occurs in the course of an account of expiations for sins in general, and the author's intention is to enjoin knowledge of Ātman as the best means by which to purify the mind of those who have committed the various sins. It is therefore clear that in the Brahmin society of that time, the knowledge of Ātman was considered capable of purifying the mind. It is to be noticed here that this Vedāntic thought is put forward as the view of the author himself and not merely as a possible view. Even by this time, Vedāntic thought had already become a philosophy of the Brahmins.

Appendix 2

THE ŚAṄKARA COMMENTARY

In a note in his *Shoki Vedānta Tetsugaku-shi* (History of Early Vedanta Philosophy), Professor Nakamura remarks that the commentary on the Ādhyatma-paṭala attributed to Śaṅkara is in his style, quoting only the older Upanishads, and the thought is consonant with his authentic works; he concludes that it is either by Śaṅkara himself or by some thinker of similar ideas who lived about the same time.

Professor Sengaku Mayeda of the University of Tōkyō has made a special study of the authenticity of important works attributed to Śaṅkara (defined as the author of the Brahma-sūtra commentary); he has not published a separate analysis of this Ādhyatma-paṭala commentary, but in his *Encyclopaedia Britannica* article on Śaṅkara, where he summarises his conclusions, he states that it is a genuine work.

In the monumental work on the history of the Dharma-Śāstra Kane notes in passing that in style and content it is probably a work of Śaṅkara.

The quotations from authority, even in this very short work, show a pattern characteristic of Śaṅkara, with the old and middle Upanishads Bṛihadāraṇyaka, Chāndogya, Muṇḍaka, Kāṭhaka and Taittirīya well to the fore; and of smṛitis the most prominent place given to Mahābhārata, especially Mokshadharma, Anugītā and the Bhagavad Gītā itself. Manu, again characteristically, has several mentions.

All these quotations can be found in one or more of Śaṅkara's commentaries, and some familiar ones occur often in the same pairings; for example two well-known texts, Bṛihad. III.7.23 'there is no other seer but this' and Chānd. VI.8.7 'thou art that', come side by side in the commentary on sutra 4 here and also paired under Brahma-sūtra II.3.30.

But there are more significant parallels, especially with the Gītā commentary, in the presentation of not particularly common texts. The following six quotations appear in close proximity at the end of the Ādhyatma-paṭala commentary introduction (where quotation is partial, the words actually quoted are italicised).

1 Renunciation alone excelled these, the lower austerities (Mahānār. 78.12) (tāni vā etānyavarāṇi tapāṃsi, nyāsa evātyarecayat); (14 words further on) ... renunciation alone excelled.

2 Not by action, not by offspring, not by wealth, (but) *by giving up some attained immortality* (Mahānār. 12.14; Kaivalya 2) (na karmṇā na prajayā dhanena *tyāgenaike amṛitatvam ānaśuḥ*).

3 There are two well-trodden paths, the first being the path of action and the other being renunciation. Of the two it is renunciation which is the higher (Taitt. X.62.12) (dvau panthānāvanunishkrāntatarau karmapathaścaivam purastāt samnyāsaśca, tayoḥ saṃnyāsa evātirecayati); (paraphrased in Mahābh. XII.233.6).

4 *Give up duty and its opposite*, both right and wrong give up; having given up both right and wrong, give up that by which you give them up (Mahābh. XII. 229.40) (*tyaja dharmam adharmaṃ ca* ubhe satyānṛite tyaja ubhe satyānṛite tyaktvā yena tyajasi tat tyaja).

5 having known, *let him practise actionlessness* (unidentified smriti) (jñātvā, *naishkarmyam acaret*) (as quoted in Aitareya comm. intro.) or: abhayam sarvabhūtebhyo dattvā *naishkarmyam acaret* (Mahābh XIV.46.18) (as quoted in Gītā III.4 comm.).

6 By action a person is bound and by knowledge he is released: *therefore* the sages who see the supreme *do no action* (Mahābh XII.233.7) (karmanā badhyate jantu vidyayā ca vimucyante tasmād karma na kurvanti, yatayaḥ paradarśinaḥ).

These texts appear in juxtaposition in a number of other places in the commentaries of Śaṅkara:

Gītā, III intro.	1 2 4 6
XVIII. 55	1 4
Bṛihad. IV.5.12:	2 3
Aitareya intro.	2 5
Iśā	2 1 3 (Mahābh. XII.233.6)

Again, at the beginning of the introduction to the Ādhyatma-paṭala, there are two quotations side by side from the Law-book itself:

(a) Having given up truth and untruth, pleasure and pain, the Vedas and this world, let him seek the Self (2.21.13) (satyānṛite sukhaduḥkhe Vedān imam lokam amuñca parityajyā 'tmānam anvicchet).

(b) Men of the several castes and orders, each devoted to his respective duties, reap the fruits of their actions after death (varṇā āsramāśca svakarme nishṭhāḥ pretya karmaphalam anubhūya) (2.2.3, also Gautama X1.29; quoted as from Gautama).

The commentary on Gītā XVIII.55 quotes (a), and (b) is quoted in the commentary to XVIII 44 and 66, as from smṛiti in both cases.

These juxtapositions of texts which are not frequently cited may be an indication – almost like finger-prints – that the works in which they appear are by the same hand. In particular it may be that the Gītā commentary and the Ādhyatma-paṭala commentary were written about the same time, when the texts were in the mind of the writer in these pairings.

There are a number of other connections with the Gītā commentary as regards quotations; for example the Rig Veda quotation which appears here under sutra 10, yen a dyaurugrā pṛithivī ca dṛihlā, occurs also in the commentary to Gītā XV.13.

It is also worth noting that the unidentified quotation from śruti appearing under sūtra 4, ākāśavat sarvagataśca nityaḥ, is not from some late Upanishad but appears in Śaṅkara's commentary on Brahma-sūtra 111.2.37; it is also, incidentally, quoted by Madhusūdana Sarasvatī in his commentary on Gītā IV.6.

Śaṅkara frequently quotes and refers to this Chapter of the Self in other works. However, even when quoting one of the verses, which he himself says are Upanishadic, he attributes them to smṛiti and not to śruti, inasmuch as the source was no longer known in his time. Sūtra 2 he quotes in his commentary to Brahma-sūtra I.1.17: ātmalābhān na paraṃ vidyate. His independent work called the Thousand Teachings has in the verse part 16.44: ātmalābhāḥ paro lābha iti śāstropapattayaḥ. In verses 4 and 5 of Ch. 17 of the same he has: ātmalābhāt para nānyo lābhaḥ kaścana vidyate; ātmalābhāt paraḥ prokto. In the commentary on Muṇḍ III.2.3 it is: sarvalābhāt parama ātmalābhāt.

In the first verse of metrical part of the Thousand Teachings appears the unusual compound guhāśaya 'lying in the cave', which occurs indeed in Muṇḍaka but applied to prāṇas, whereas in the Chapter of the Self it is Ātman. In the prose section (I.38) Śaṅkara quotes the sūtra explicitly – pūḥ prāṇinaḥ guhāśayasya.

One of the tests for texts ascribed to Śaṅkara is the use of terms expressing Ignorance in his technical sense. In this Chapter of the Self, it is ajñāna which is the seed of doshas (sarvadosha-bīja-bhūtam-ajñānam – sūtra 3) which cause saṃsāra, and elsewhere avidyā is only one of these. (The Gītā commentary has compounds like avidyādidoshaih, IX.8 and avidyādidoshavattva, XIII.2). But in the introduction, avidyā is the cause of saṃsāra. And under sūtras 10 and 11, he describes doshas as born of mithyā-pratyaya (mithyāpratyayabhava), preceded by it (mithyāpratyayapiirvaka), accompanied by it (mithyāpratyayasacivat), and in the introduction, accompanied by mithyā-jñāna (samithyajñāna). Perhaps the idea is similar to that in the yoga sūtra, where avidyā is the first from which the other doshas spring, being pervaded by it, though there the term is kleśa (following the sūtra), as however also in the Gītā commentary on VI.27 (mohādi-kleśa). But avidyā is not among the doshas listed in sūtra 13: moha does appear, but Śaṅkara does not take the opportunity of glossing it as avidyā.

In general in the Chapter of the Self, vidyā, brahmavidyā, and jñāna are synonymous as the means to destroy avidyā or ajñāna, and it can be supposed that these two last, and mithyā-jñāna (and mithyā-pratyaya as in the Brahma-sūtra commentary) are the same, as for Śaṅkara in the Gītā commentary (though not for his followers, for whom avidyā is not mithyā-jñāna but the cause of it).

In doctrine, the Chapter of the Self is close to one main teaching of Śaṅkara's Gītā commentary, though not identical with it. This is, that liberation is not necessarily from Knowledge alone, but from devotion-to-Knowledge (jñāna-nishṭhā) together with renunciation of all works (introduction to Gita: sarvakarmasaṃnyāsa-purvakād ātma-jñāna-nishṭhā-rūpād dharmād). In this system, jñāna-prāpti may merely qualify the aspirant for jñāna-nishṭhā which consists in *devotion* to that Knowledge, spontaneously entailing samnyāsa. The process of jñāna-nishṭhā is described, according to Śaṅkara, in a number of places in the Gītā: II.54–72, V.17–26, all Ch. VI, XII. 13–20, XIII.7–18, XIV.23–5, XVIII.51–5. The Chapter of the Self commentary refers specifically to II.59, and to the passage of chapter

XIV. The descriptions are mostly in negative terms, but he reads into all of them a positive injunction to practise samādhi on Self or the Lord. The whole tenor of the commentary, however, is that the – apparently – enjoined seclusion, renunciation, and even meditation, are in practice *natural* results of the Knowledge which he already has; the injunction to meditate on Self is in reality only restrictive, to rule out distractions; free from distractions, meditation on Self follows naturally. The doctrine is summed up in many places; for instance II.69 says that when they have realised the Self (quoting V.17 – tadbuddhayas tadātmanas), their duty (adhikāra) consists in renunciation of all action and devotion to Knowledge (jñāna-nishṭhā). And there is no need of a specific injunction to meditate on Ātman, for the reason that Ātman is one's own very Self. Hence it is natural to do so.

That the jñāna with which jñāna-nishṭhā begins is not merely theoretical is clear from the many instances where it is glossed as samyag-darśana or paramārthadarśana (e.g. IV.41; V.6, 8, 9, 13, 26; IX.22; XII.5, 12 etc.).

In the Gītā commentary, however, Śaṅkara allows certain exceptions to the rule that jñāna-nishṭhā must entail saṃnyāsa; to set an example to the world, to protect the people, to avoid the censure of the 'orthodox' (śishṭa – presumably followers of Manu who held that the stages of life must be gone through in succession) or simply 'something preventing it' (IV.19). In the commentary to IV.2, several kings who were practising jñāna-nishṭhā are given as examples. In this respect the Chapter of the Self commentary follows the principle that there may be exceptions to the inevitability of saṃnyāsa.

Śaṅkara states explicitly, in his commentary on Gītā III.16, that the teaching is based on Bṛihad. III.5.1, and it may be significant that his quotation is in fact a paraphrase of it, bringing out his doctrine:

The Brahmins, *having known* this the Self and free from illusory knowledge (mithyā-jñāna), awakening from all desires for sons, etc. cherished inevitably by those still under illusion, lead a wandering life begging for necessities. They have nothing else to do than resort to devotion to Self-knowledge (ātmajñānanishṭhā).

The word 'kārya' (something to do) implies action.

In the commentary on this passage in the original Upanishad, he uses two of the key words of the Chapter of the Self: yogī and paṇḍita. He sums up its doctrine here:

What a Brahman-Knower should do is to eliminate all ideas of the non-Self; doing this he accomplishes his task and becomes a yogī. After having known fully the paṇḍitahood which is Self-knowledge, and the strength which is elimination of ideas of the non-Self, he knows about meditation ... He becomes a Brahman-Knower ... his status as a Brahman-Knower is literally true.

The same doctrine of Knowledge being reinforced, or rather protected from disturbance of remaining prārabdhakarma, by yogas like inner and outer control, giving up, and samādhi practice, is found in the commentaries on Brahma-sūtra III.4.20, Muṇḍaka III.2.6, and the Thousand Teachings prose part I.4. In this last, three recommendations are made for 'making firm' the Knowledge of a paramahaṃsa renunciate: Angerlessness and the other (yogas of the Chapter of the Self), ahiṃsā and the other yama and niyama qualifications (of the yoga-sūtra), and humility and the other (qualities of Gītā XIII.7–11). But these practices (though they may be referred to as karma) are not something alien to Knowledge – they are 'grounding in Brahman' as explained in the comments to Brahma-sūtra III.4.20.

The doctrine of the Chapter of the Self is summed up in a sentence in the third chapter of the prose part of the Thousand Teachings: 'A Knower (vidvān) who is tormented by the objects perceived, should practise parisankhyāna meditation.' This meditation begins with separation of Self, which is by nature Seeing, from all objects, as in the system of Patañjali, but it ends with a declaration of non-duality, 'Nothing exists except Ātman'. This takes it further than the prasankhyana meditation of the yoga-sūtra, which stops at Isolation and does not deny duality.

The path of jñāna-nishṭhā is simply Knowledge. In the debate in the Gītā commentary on XVIII.55 an objector points out that a thing is known by knowledge, and to say it is known by devotion-to-knowledge (jñāna-nishṭhā) is meaningless; the reply is, that devotion-to-knowledge merely means that the knowledge is freed from obstacles by practice of humility, one-pointed meditation and the others listed in XIII.7–11.

A special and valuable point in the presentation in the Chapter of the Self is, that it reconciles the apparent contradiction that though knowledge alone is to be the means of liberation, at the same time yogas are enjoined. It is explained that some Knowers attain Brahman fully at once, while in others the clarity of Knowledge is obscured by doshas thrown up by karma-already-in-operation. The yogas are intended for the latter.

In the same way, the Thousand Teachings metrical part, IV.3 states that karma-already-in-operation overpowers Brahman-Knowledge, but only for a time, till the Brahman-Knowledge is as firm as the ordinary knowledge of the body as the self. If this commentary is authentic, as seems very probable, it is an important guide to Śaṅkara's thought. Though he is following a text, it is not one of those on which he might have felt more or less obliged to comment (more likely might have been some section of Manu, for whom he had such reverence); he must have chosen it because it expressed his own ideas. Looking at the sūtras, he could easily have interpreted 'having thrown off the doshas' as practice of yogas only *before* Knowledge, with Peace following Knowledge immediately in all cases. But his commentary explains at length that yoga practice leads up to Knowledge, and then (in some cases, where necessary) also follows it, before liberation is attained. In this he follows his Gītā doctrine, in which samādhi-practice is one of the elements of karma-yoga leading up to Knowledge (II.39), is the immediate means to Knowledge (VI.intro.) and is jñāna-nishṭhā practised after the rise of Knowledge (XVIII.52).

There are a couple of minor points where comparisons can be made with other works of Śaṅkara. Under sūtras 7 and 10, he refers to the projection in order of the five elements, from Space to Earth, and their dissolution into each other in reverse order. The text does not require him to introduce the doctrine, and he does it voluntarily as he does in the first chapter of the prose part of the Thousand Teachings. Professor Mayeda has published a study of Śaṅkara's cosmology, and he comments in a letter,

As far as I can see, the author's idea in these two sūtras does not show any essential difference from that of the author of the Brahma-sūtra-bhāṣya. In neither case is the theory of pañcīkaraṇa explicitly set out, but the author seems to hold a kind of pañcīkaraṇa, accepting the five gross elements. This fact cannot be a strong evidence of Śaṅkara's authorship of the Vivaraṇa, but it may be one of the pointers to it as you remark.

I am grateful to Professor Mayeda for this opinion, which must carry great weight. I should also say how much I have relied upon his studies on the authenticity of the Śaṅkara commentaries on the Gītā, the Thousand Teachings, the Kenopanishad and Māṇḍukya Kārikas, and his analysis of Jñāna and Karman as means to moksha. The Chapter of the Self commentary agrees in general with the cycle of saṃsāra set out in the Thousand Teachings, especially verses 3 and 4 of the first chapter of the metrical part, but there is an interesting difference. In the Thousand Teachings, the cycle is:

1 karmas as the result of actions in previous lives
2 connection with a body
3 experience of pleasure and pain
4 passion and aversion (which are doshas, as in verse 7)
5 action (kriyā) (of)
6 dharma and a-dharma
7 connection with a body again as a result

But the Chapter of the Self makes the karmas from previous lives bring up doshas (i.e. 4) *before* the experience of pleasure and pain (3). The reason given is that there cannot be experience of pleasure and pain unless there is already some desire or aversion in the experiencer.

List of Illustrations

Acknowledgments

My grateful thanks goes to Professor Hajime Nakamura, who went over the translation of the main text in detail with me in Tokyo, giving me the benefit of his wonderful knowledge of the whole field, and also agreed to publication here of a translation of the section on the Chapter of the Self from his History of Early Vedanta. Professor Nakamura also advised me on the translation of parts of the Shankara commentary on the Yoga Sutras.

I am most grateful to Professor Sengaku Mayeda of Tokyo University for tracing some of the difficult references, and for his comments on the authenticity of the Shankara commentary, a field in which he has specialised. These are included in the notes in Appendix 2.

I also record my appreciation to Ken Speyer, who first took me through this commentary.

Grateful acknowledgments are due to His Holiness Sri Jagadguru Shankaracharya, and officials of the temple at Śṛingeri for supplying the photographs used in the text, to Professor Hamano for obtaining the photograph taken by the Japanese-Indian Nanda Devi Expedition used for the frontispiece, and to Shanti Sadan (publishers) for permission to quote from Dr Hari Prasad Shastri's *Heart of the Eastern Mystical Teaching.*

By The Same Author

A First Zen Reader
A Second Zen Reader (The Tiger's Cave)
Zen and the Ways
Realisation of the Supreme Self
The Complete Commentary by Shankara on the Yoga Sutras
The Chapter of the Self
Jewels from the Indra Net
Three Ages of Zen
Samurai Zen (The Warrior Koans)
The Old Zen Master
Fingers and Moons
Encounters in Yoga and Zen
Lotus Lake, Dragon Pool
The Dragon Mask
The Spirit of Budo
Japanese Chess (Shogi, Japan's game of Strategy)
Kata Judo
Championship Judo